William Andrews

The Church Treasury

Of History, Custom, Folk-lore, etc

William Andrews

The Church Treasury
Of History, Custom, Folk-lore, etc

ISBN/EAN: 9783744779043

Printed in Europe, USA, Canada, Australia, Japan

Cover: Foto ©Lupo / pixelio.de

More available books at **www.hansebooks.com**

The Church Treasury

of

History, Custom, Folk-Lore, etc.

Edited by

William Andrews.

LONDON:
WILLIAM ANDREWS & CO., 5, FARRINGDON AVENUE.

1898.

Preface.

THIS volume of new studies on old subjects is sent forth with a hope that it will form an acceptable contribution to the history of the Church of England.

My thanks are tendered to my contributors for their valuable co-operation cheerfully given. Special mention must be made of my friend, the Rev. Geo. S. Tyack, B.A., who has written largely for my pages, and has ever been ready to assist me in solving obscure points in my studies.

Mr. Chas. J. Clark, publisher, London, has kindly placed at my disposal the charming pictures which appear on pages 37 and 41; the Rev. Francis Haslewood, F.S.A., the one inserted on page 203; the Rev. J. B. Clare, B.A., the one which appears on page 217; and to these gentlemen I am greatly obliged. The illustrations of the article by Mr. T. Tindall Wildridge are mainly from his own drawings.

In conclusion I have only to add that if the work wins a welcome similar to that accorded to my previous productions, prepared on the same plan, I shall have every reason to feel grateful.

WILLIAM ANDREWS.

THE HULL PRESS.

Contents.

	PAGE
STAVE-KIRKS. By the Rev. Geo. S. Tyack, B.A.	1
CURIOUS CHURCHES IN CORNWALL. By the Rev. W. S. Lach-Szyrma, M.A.	21
HOLY WELLS. By Cuming Walters	29
HERMITS AND HERMIT-CELLS. By the Rev. J. Hudson Barker, B.A.	68
CHURCH WAKES	97
FORTIFIED CHURCH TOWERS. By William Andrews	105
THE KNIGHTS TEMPLARS: THEIR CHURCHES AND THEIR PRIVILEGES. By J. Rogers Rees	112
ENGLISH MEDIÆVAL PILGRIMAGES. By W. H. Thompson	129
PILGRIMS' SIGNS. By the Rev. Geo. S. Tyack, B.A.	145
HUMAN SKIN ON CHURCH DOORS. By the Rev. Geo. S. Tyack, B.A.	158
ANIMALS OF THE CHURCH, IN WOOD, STONE, AND BRONZE. By T. Tindall Wildridge	168
QUERIES IN STONES. By the Rev. Francis Haslewood, F.S.A.	201
PICTURES IN CHURCHES. By the Rev. Geo. S. Tyack, B.A.	205
FLOWERS AND THE RITES OF THE CHURCH. By the Rev. Hilderic Friend	227
GHOST-LAYERS AND GHOST-LAYING. By the Rev. R. Wilkins Rees	241
CHURCH WALKS. By the Rev. W. B. Russell Caley, M.A.	269
THE WESTMINSTER WAX-WORKS. By William Andrews	275
INDEX	297

THE CHURCH TREASURY.

Stave=Kirks.

By Rev. G. S. Tyack, B.A.

IN architecture, "wood should be used externally only on the smallest and least monumental class of buildings," and that from the fact that it is "dark in colour, liable to warp and split, and combustible." So we read in a standard work on the art, and the propriety of the statement will be generally admitted. Yet in any primitive society, surrounded by abundant growing timber, and supplied only with rude tools, wood must almost invariably be more commonly used as a building material than stone or brick. Its readiness to hand, the comparative ease of working it, and, when wrought into serviceable lengths, of transporting it, would all be arguments in its favour; while its want of durability would be little felt by a race, which, having no certain records of a remote past, was correspondingly unaccustomed to provide for a distant future.

It would be a mistake, however, to conclude that only people in the rudest state reared wooden buildings. In every country, and at every time, the country districts, remote from the wealth and from the art of the more populous centres, are compelled by want of means, in cases where the resources of the peasantry only can be relied upon, to employ such local materials as are the cheapest; and in their simplicity they are content therewith. Thus it happens that in every land that was, or is, rich in forests, we find traces of timber erections in the past, and even in the present instances of them, more or less numerous in proportion as the growth of civilization has left untouched the simple tastes of the people, and the spread of population has not encroached upon the primeval woods.

The building of wooden churches is, perhaps, the most striking illustration of this position, in that the faithful of all times and climes have been wont to bestow upon their sanctuaries the highest efforts of their art. Yet the earliest Christians of Cyrene, situated as they were amid the deserts of Libya, far removed from quarries, or indeed from trees of any magnitude, built or wove their churches, according to the testimony of Sulpicius

Severus, at the beginning of the fifth century, of small rods or withes.

Similarly we are not surprised to find in countries like Norway and Russia, countries no less noted for the abundance of their forests than for the primitive simplicity of their peasantry, that wooden churches are far from being uncommon even to this day, although they are now rapidly giving place to more durable structures.

In the former country there are several examples dating from the eleventh and twelfth centuries, and of a quaintly barbaric style of architecture. One at Urnes is remarkable for having on its external timbers much characteristic runic carving, such as is frequently found on monumental stones in northern Europe, but has survived in wood only in this, and a few other Norwegian churches. Urnes Church measures only sixty-five feet by twenty-four, and in this respect is not greatly different from the other village churches of the same class, all being but small. The largest, and one of the most curious of them, is at Hitterdal, and measures eighty-seven feet by fifty-seven. Its extraordinary conglomeration of roofs, pinnacles, and gables, is utterly unlike anything civil or ecclesiastical with which the rest of the western world is familiar, and suggests a Chinese pagoda rather than a Christian church. A still more fantastic example is at Burgund.

The wooden churches of Russia, of which there are many in the villages, are constructed, like Canadian log-huts, of round logs laid one on another horizontally, the only dignified feature of their exterior being the bulb-shaped dome, found everywhere in the country, from the cathedrals of the Kremlin, to the humblest hamlet church. There is a good mediæval example near Kostroma, in Eastern Russia, where the aisles are separated from the nave by wooden pillars with square capitals, the nave itself being covered with a "waggon" roof.

Turning now to our own country, and recalling the fact that it, too, was once clothed with wide-spreading forests, and inhabited even in Christian times by a simple-minded people, whose intercourse with the more cultured continent was but slight, we rather expect than otherwise to find evidence of an equally primitive style of architecture. And the evidence forthcoming is abundant.

In Roman Britain, as we know, there were

some few stone churches, for we have probable remains of them in Canterbury and at Dover; but it is noteworthy that such remains are confined to the south-east corner of the country, where

HITTERDAL CHURCH, NORWAY.

continental influence would be most felt. The Venerable Bede speaks of a time "when there was not a stone church in all the land, but the custom was to build them all of wood." It may be that his statement is too sweeping, but doubtless it was literally true of Northern England and Southern Scotland, the districts with which the saintly monk of Jarrow was most intimately familiar.

Legend has it that the first Christian church built in the island was a wattle shed, erected by S. Joseph of Arimathæa at Glastonbury; and another legend tells of a church made of boughs only, wherein lay the body of S. Cuthbert, until so much of the stately Cathedral of Durham was completed as to allow of his relics being translated thither. The site of the earlier shrine, immediately beneath the east-front of the cathedral, is still occupied by a little church, S. Mary-le-bow, that is, according to this rather doubtful derivation, S. Mary of the boughs.

More definite evidence is borne by our early ecclesiastical historians. Bede tells us that Edwin, King of Northumbria, having been converted by the preaching of S. Paulinus, "was baptized at York, on the holy day of Easter (A.D. 627), being the 12th day of April, in the Church of S. Peter the Apostle, which he himself had built of timber, whilst he was being catechised and instructed for baptism. In that city also he appointed the seat of the bishopric of his teacher and bishop, Paulinus. But as soon as he was baptized, he took care, by the advice of the said Paulinus, to build in the same place a larger and nobler church of stone, in the midst whereof that same oratory which he had first erected should be enclosed."

The same writer records that when Finan succeeded S. Aidan in 652 as Bishop of Lindisfarne, he built a church in the island; "Yet, after the manner of the Scots, he made it, not of stone, but of hewn oak, and covered it with reeds." Subsequently Eadbert, who became bishop in 688, "took off the thatch, and covered it, both roof and walls, with plates of lead."

William of Malmsbury makes mention of a wooden church, or stave-kirk, as the old English name was, at Dutlinge, in Somersetshire; and of the same material were reared the earliest monastic establishments of the country with their churches. Ingulphus tells us that Croyland Abbey was originally built of logs and planks, joined and worked with great skill and accuracy, and roofed with lead. King Alfred's abbey-church at Aethelingey was of timber; and King Edgar in a charter granted to Malmsbury Abbey, expresses his intention, as a thank-offering for the prosperity given him by God, of restoring "the sacred monasteries in which, they being composed of rotten shingles and worm-eaten boards, divine service was neglected." Canute granted a charter in 1032 to the Abbey of Glastonbury, which was given "in the wooden church in the King's presence."

The nomenclature of a few places seems to point to the existence of stave-kirks. The venerable Bede explains the name of Whitherne, or White House (Candida Casa), in Galloway, by the fact that S. Ninian built there a stone church, the whiteness of the newly-cut stone being in marked contrast to the darker timber structures with which the folk were familiar. S. Ninian, who built this church in 397, had been educated in Rome, and was the friend of S. Martin of Tours; hence his knowledge of the use of stone was gained abroad, and he is even said to have obtained masons from Tours to undertake the work. In Cheshire and in Kent we have villages named Woodchurch, and in Yorkshire a Woodkirk, both of which terms, although they may possibly mean the "Church in the wood," seem more probably to point to the existence of wooden churches, perhaps at a time sufficiently late to make them somewhat remarkable.

Another illustration of the prevalence in primitive times of wooden architecture is provided by early stone work, which is formed on obviously wooden designs. There are tombs in Egypt whose walls are simply a reproduction of square beams placed side by side perpendicularly, and others in Lycia in which the very mortices and pins of a timber structure are imitated in the more durable material. But examples more cognate to our subject are supplied by some of the church towers of Saxon times. The fine tower of Earl's Barton Church, in Northamptonshire, is a case in point. The long pilaster-like slips and the

CHURCH TOWER, EARL'S BARTON.

transverse bars distinctly suggest the bracing of a timber building, and the balusters of the windows look far more like the work of the turner than of the mason. Somewhat similar "turned" work may be seen in the doorway of Monkwearmouth Church, erected in the seventh century by Benedict Biscop, and the "timber-bracing" decoration occurs again in the tower of S. Peter's, at Barton-on-Humber, Lincolnshire. It thus appears evident that our forefathers were so far familiar with stave-kirks of some pretentions to size and dignity, that even when intercourse with the continent had taught them to rise a step higher in architectural art and to build in stone, it was still some time before they could throw aside the models to which custom had wedded them, and before they learnt the capabilities of the new material.

Records are found of the existence of stave-kirks in various places, besides those very early ones to which reference has been made. Domesday Book tells of one at Bigland, in Yorkshire, and there were others at North Elmham and at Shernbourn, in Norfolk. A wooden chapel survived at Bury S. Edmund's until 1303; S. Aldhelm's, Durham, standing in 998, the Ladye Chapel at Tykford, and that at Spalding so late as 1059, were all of wood; as also, to name a continental instance, was S. Stephen's at Mayence in 1011.

So far no allusion has been made to existing examples of the stave-kirk in England, yet there are several such, among which the right of priority

GREENSTEAD CHURCH, A.D. 1013 (AS IT WAS IN 1748)
"*Vetusta Monumenta.*"

on the grounds both of antiquity and interest must be given to the little Church of Greenstead, in Essex. This curious survival of a distant age is said to have been constructed in the first place as a temporary shrine for the relics of S. Edmund, the king and martyr. The story of the various translations of these relics brings to our notice more than one wooden church. The saintly king was done to death by the heathen Danes on the 20th day of November, 870, and his body was first laid to rest in a wooden chapel at Hoxne in Suffolk, where it lay "in terra defossus" until 903, when it was taken, as yet untainted by decay, to a splendid shrine in a larger wooden church at Bedrichesworth, thenceforth known as Bury S. Edmunds. Another incursion of the Danes under Turkill, in 1010, drove the monks of Bury from their house, and they took with them in their flight to London, as the most precious of their possessions the relics of Edmund the "kyng, martyr, and virgyne." Three years later they were able to make their way back to their monastery along the ancient road which ran from London to Bury through Oldford, Abridge, Stapleford, Greenstead, Dunmow, and Clare; and it was during this journey that, according to an apparently well-grounded tradition, the wooden shrine at Greenstead was erected. The manuscript *Life and Passion of Saint Edmund* (now in Lambeth Palace Library) asserts that "a certain resting-place near Stapleford received his body on its return from London," and another ancient account says that it "rested near Aungre (Chipping Ongar), where a wooden chapel remains to this day in memory of S. Edmund."

The original chapel was only twenty-nine feet nine inches long by fourteen feet wide. A few courses of brick form the groundwork, and on these are placed rough-hewn timbers, consisting of half-logs placed perpendicularly. At the top these logs are cut away to thin edges which fit into a groove in upper transverse beams which bear the roof. The wood is still sound though so time-worn that authorities differ as to its being oak or chestnut. The tower, built of horizontal timbers is of a later date, and the brick chancel dates only from Tudor times. There is no sign of any window having been allowed for in the original building, the former windows in the roof, with the present roof, being no part of the pre-Norman structure. There may have been an east window, which was removed when the chancel was added; or, if the little chapel was at first intended only as a temporary shelter for the body of S. Edmund, it may have been actually windowless at the first. The porch and two stout buttresses are also modern additions to this simplest of churches, which evidently had in its first state no attempt at decoration of any kind.

In Cheshire are several important and interesting examples of stave-kirks, although none can compete with Greenstead in antiquity. Lower Peover has one dating from the days of Henry II., formed of crossed timbers and plaster-

LOWER PEOVER CHURCH.

work. It has a nave and aisles, and a chancel with aisles, the tower alone not being of timber. Marton Church, built in the fourteenth century, does not admit even of this exception, being wholly of wood; oak columns separate the nave from the aisles, and oak arches bear up the timbers of the roof. The belfry, within which hang three bells dating respectively from 1598, 1663, and 1758, is a most skilful application of the material employed to the necessary purposes of stability and strength.

Chadkirk, also in Cheshire, was probably originally a building of similar construction, but in successive alterations and repairs stone has pushed out the earlier wood, though the porch,

MARTON CHURCH.

the bell-cote, and most of the east wall are still of wood, and the east window retains its wooden mullions.

We open a wide field, however, when we touch on churches partially of wood. In former times the English carpenters,—artists in wood they might more strictly be called—were pre-eminent, as witness some of the splendid wooden roofs, and other architectural details that have come down to our own days. The roofs of Peterborough and Ely cathedrals, the stalls at Salisbury, the dean's cloisters at Windsor, the screens in the Palace Chapel at Chichester, and in S. John's Hospital, Winchester, all amply attest the skill of the English craftsman in bygone days. It was

CHADKIRK CHURCH.

natural, therefore, that such skill should frequently have been called into play in those, and other ways, in the building of churches.

In Essex we find some striking instances of wooden spires. At Blackmore is one built in three diminishing stages, the two upper ones of timber, laid horizontally in the topmost, and

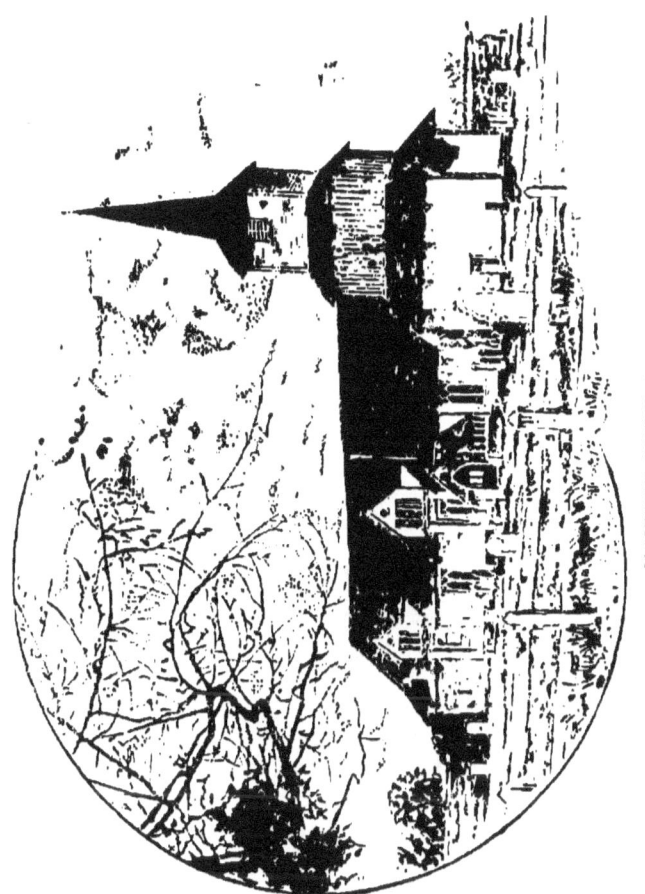

BLACKMORE CHURCH, ESSEX.

STAVE-KIRKS.

perpendicularly in the middle stage. Each storey has a projecting roof, and the whole is crowned with a spire. Antiquaries have suggested that the tower of the neighbouring church of Margaretting may have been designed by the same architect, the external form being to some extent similar, and the internal arrangement of timbers so as to secure the utmost strength being equally ingenious. Stock Church, also in Essex, has another instance of a cleverly constructed wooden tower.

Ribbesford, in Worcestershire, has wooden arcades in the nave; and the churches of Newland, in the same county, and of Newtown in Montgomeryshire, are both largely of wood. The number of wooden porches and lychgates of the country, many of them excellent in design, is legion.

TIMBER WORK OF TOWER OF MARGARETTING CHURCH.

Many of our stave-kirks were doubtless taken down to make way for noble structures of stone, but naturally the action of the weather on timbers not always perfectly seasoned has destroyed many, and fire has accounted for the destruction of not a few. The knowledge that most of the churches of the time were but wooden buildings will explain the wholesale burning of them, which the Danish marauders accomplished apparently so easily, when they descended on the eastern counties. And the wonder is that so many traces of the simple stave-kirks of our forefathers should have weathered so succesfully the storms of time.

Curious Churches of Cornwall.

By Rev. W. S. Lach-Szyrma, M.A.

THERE are few counties in England where we can better study the past in the present than in Cornwall. Side by side we see the last improvements in machinery in the mines, and the monuments of the most remote antiquity, perhaps, the new school of antiquaries say, as old as the Father of History, or indeed a great deal older, for they belong to the Bronze or later Stone age —before the Aryan Celts had come to this part of Western Europe, and when a sort of broad-headed Lappish savages inhabited the Cornish moorlands and the English forests. In fact, in Cornwall you find remains which elsewhere in England are curious and very rare indeed. Why?

1. The granite of Cornwall is one of the most enduring of stones. What is made of it may last, with decent treatment, two or three thousand years in excellent condition. So the cromlechs, the hut circles, the menhirs of the aboriginal Euskarians of Britain remain in admirable condition, though perhaps older than Rome itself, or

the dawn of ancient Greek civilization; and still more, Christian antiquities made in granite may be expected to survive.

2. The people, until recent times, had a strong prejudice against injuring antiquities or ancient remains. Of course this was most intense with regard to Christian antiquities, but certainly the peasants have often preserved the secular remains of the "old men" for fear of being "ill-wished." Hundreds of useful evidences of the past have therefore been handed down to us from this reason; and in church matters not only stone carving, but wood work and stained glass have been well preserved for our age. One chief advantage Cornwall has, is that Puritanism and iconoclasm was never very strong there. In the seventeenth century, there was not much harm done to ancient monuments or churches. Causes at work in other counties did not avail here.

First among the curious churches in Cornwall, we will consider St. Neot—five miles from Liskeard. It is a wonderful old-world place, where one can dream of the Middle Ages, and see the thoughts and feelings of the Merrie England of the Middle Ages, not in mere representation like the unreal Old London, or Old

CURIOUS CHURCHES OF CORNWALL. 23

Manchester of exhibitions, but in mediæval work, partly done by fifteenth century artists. The windows of St. Neot have few rivals of their kind in England, and were very fairly restored some time ago. They are fifteen in number, and represent :—

1. The Life of St. George—the patron of England.
2. The Life of St. Neot, the local saint.
3. A group of Cornish saints in the Young Women's window.
4. The Creation.
5. Some Old Testament scenes.

The work is rough, and South Kensington might not quite approve of some of the drawing, but it is archaic, quaint, in parts devotional, and thoroughly mediæval in spirit. Each window has a name and a title, probably from its origin, and each window is a study in itself. In the St. George's windows we have the wonderful adventures of the saint, *e.g.*, his fighting, his killing the dragon, his being taken prisoner by the Gauls, his torments and martyrdom.

St. George held an important position in the popular life of English patrin in the past, and the war cry "St. George and Merrie England," and the cross of St. George, still inscribed in our Union Jack, and carried to every colony and over every sea, waving in every battlefield of English soldiers, and on every British ship, attests the power of the St. George legend (possibly a myth of the victory of Christianity over evil) in the England of the past. Here it stands, storied in quaint form, in rich colouring on the painted glass. The St. George legend was a living thing in popular life in Cornwall, as in other English counties. There, as well as in Dorset and Yorkshire, the drama of " St. George and the Turkish Knight " was performed even to our own times. I have seen it myself acted, not many miles from St. Neot at Christmastide, by the Cornish miners, but believe it has now (like many other harmless and picturesque customs) died out before Board Schools and Methodism (which looked on it as "carnal and popish.")

The St. Noet legend is of less general, but more local interest. It contains some quaint animal legends, and brings us into contact with some of the strange ideas of our mediæval ancestors.

If the interior of St. Noet brings so vividly before us the home life and popular thought of mediæval England, the exterior of St. Austell is only a little less instructive. In most of our old parish churches the niches we have were fitted with figures, but iconoclasm has ruined them all. St. Austell seems in the old time to have been a place outside popular movements, and forgotten by Puritans and iconoclasts. Now it has become a centre of life, but the old statues in the niches, and especially the remarkable symbol of the Blessed Trinity on the tower shows us what scores of old English parish churches were like in the olden time.

If the windows of St. Neot are wonderful, the frescoes of Breage are almost as striking. They are only of recent discovery, *i.e.*, in 1890. The most remarkable is a huge figure of our Blessed Saviour, whose precious blood is depicted as flowing over the various implements of industry, *e.g.*, the reaping hook, scythe, shuttle, cart. This is supposed to imply the sanctification of human labour by the Incarnation—a most important doctrine. There is also a gigantic fresco of St. Christopher some 12 feet high, also of smaller ones of St. Coventin, St. Mylor, St. Germo (the patron of the adjacent parish), and St. Michael the Archangel. In every way Breage is a charming old place with fine air and scenery. It is not, as yet, sufficiently known to tourists.

The legend of the patron is that she was an Irish princess, sister of King Germo, who was induced by St. Patrick to accept Christianity; full of enthusiasm, he gave up his kingdom, was consecrated a bishop, and then went as a missionary in West Cornwall, taking his sister, St. Breaca with him, who here seems to have founded a religious house. It is interesting to find that one of the best working guilds for women is at St. Breage, a continuation of the old religious house for women. St. Breaca is said to have acted as a midwife to her female converts, but St. Germo or Germochus, was revered as an ex-king by his people. St. Germo's chair (probably of a far later date than his, *i.e.*, 450) was probably a tradition of the stone throne on which the voluntarily exiled monarch sat. The whole legend is held by some critics to be suspiciously like that of Gautama Buddha in India, but is none the less interesting to folk-lorists on that ground. St. Germo is supposed to have lived about 450, *i.e.*, over a century before Augustine landed at Ebb's fleet in Kent—in fact as far removed from his time as the age of George II. is from our day.

The westernmost and the southernmost churches in England, *i.e.*, Sennen and Landewednack, in which parishes the Land's End and Lizard are contained, both are curious churches worth seeing. Sennen has a quaint fresco of New Jerusalem, a headless statue of St. John the Baptist, and a font with a date on it, not common in the Middle Ages. In Landewednack we have a church partly built of serpentine.

At Buryan, we have what is said to be a memorial church, reared by King Athelstan as a thanksgiving for his conquest of Cornwall, and a place from which he saw the Scilly Isles. Here is a grand screen, beautifully painted, of the early Renaissance period. What a wealth of beauty there must have been in those mediæval screens. In Devon and Cornwall, those we have make us wish that more had been preserved.

Gunwallo church is built near the sea, in a quaint position. It is said to have been vowed to God by a merchant in peril of the sea, and marks the first place of land he reached. In Gwennap, we have a campanile near the church. At Paul, we have a church on English soil burnt by the Spaniards in 1595, and famous as the only churchyard in Europe which marks the death place of a language. The old Cornish language died out in this parish in the last century. The last person who professed to speak it fluently was Dolly Pentreath, of Mousehole, in this parish. A tomb was erected to her memory by Prince Lucien Bonaparte. The subject of how the language died out, and of whether Dolly Pentreath knew as much of the old tongue as she professed, has been much discussed. We cannot deal with the question here, but we believe it is without doubt that the last persons who spoke Cornish are buried in Paul churchyard, and that it is certainly the only death place of a language in England, and probably in Europe (as where and how the old Prussian and other extinct tongues died out is not quite certain). With this death place of a European tongue we leave the curious churches of Cornwall, advising our readers when they have the chance to see these old Cornish churches for themselves. They well repay a visit.

Holy Wells.

By Cuming Walters.

THAT water should be regarded by primitive man with a species of reverence is easily explicable. Whether it be the sea, the rivers, or the deep cool wells, we find the savage and the semi-civilised races regarding them with superstitious awe, and not unfrequently designating them as divinities. In the age of myths every river had its presiding goddess and its nymphs, to whom oblations were due. Various pleasing legends arose from this initial idea, only one of which we may now stay to notice, inasmuch as we are able to quote Milton's fine lines in illustrating the point. We refer to the legend of Sabrina and the river Severn, told in the luxurious lines of "Comus," wherein the nymph is depicted as swaying "smooth Severn stream" with "moist curb," in consequence of which—

> "The shepherds at their festivals
> Carol her goodness loud in rustic lays,
> And throw sweet garland wreaths into her stream
> Of pansies, pinks, and gaudy daffodils."

Some early tribes venerated the rivers as their chief or only deities; others simply regarded them as the abodes or the refuges of the gods. The Swedes believed that the Pagan gods fled to the rivers when defeated by Christianity.

The savage, investing everything in nature with personality, peopled the wells and streams with benign or malignant spirits as his mood or fancy dictated. Christianity did no more than substitute the name of a saint for the indigenous water-kelpie, and Chad, Winifred, Margaret, Catherine, Anthony, and many others figured in the place of the early myths.

Thus, one of the most curious and interesting chapters in history is that which shows how the shrewd Christian missionaries of old grafted Pagan customs upon the religion they brought over. Christianity borrowed from heathendom for purposes of good policy, and the wells at which idolatry had flourished, were transformed into the shrines of saints. The old gods were supplanted, and yet no violence was done to a faith to which early man clung with the utmost tenacity. In the records of hagiology we find with what consummate skill and ingenuity the missionaries worked, purging the wells of supposed demons, consecrating them to higher and more beneficent uses, inspiring a grateful and reverent regard in their virtues, and making them the means of keeping alive the names of the saints of the church. None of the reformers worked harder to achieve this object than Cuthbert, Columba, and Chad. The task was made easier by the undoubted healing and sanative powers of the wells; the prophets were not preaching a vain thing. Even in the grossest of the water-superstitions there is an underlying truth, and nature's marvels when rendered into folk-lore become the outward signs and manifestations of good and evil deities. There is no folly in primitive creeds, only in the incomplete and limited expression of them. Behind all shadowy and grotesque superstitions lies the primal law, the original truth, recognized by the child-mind of undeveloped man.

"When wells were dedicated to Christian saints," writes Mr. Jas. M. Mackinlay (in "Folk-lore of Scottish Lochs and Springs"), "the latter were usually considered the guardians of the sacred water. This was natural enough. If, for instance, St. Michael was supposed to watch over a spring, why should not his aid have been sought in connection with any wished-for cure? It is interesting, however, to note that this was not so in every instance. In many cases the favourite, because favourable, time for visiting a sacred spring was not the festival of the saint to whom it was dedicated, but a day quite distinct from such festival. Petitions, too, were frequently addressed not to the saint of the well, but to a character possessing fewer Christian attributes. All this points to the fact that the origin of well-worship is to be sought, not in the legends of mediæval Christianity, but in the crude fancies of an earlier Paganism."

Water is, moreover, the symbol of purity, and from very ancient times its use in connection with religious ceremonies can be traced. The lustral or purifying water was prescribed both for private and public acts of sanctification, and to this day the holy water, blest by the priest, enters largely into the rites of the Roman Catholic and the Oriental churches. The ordinances of the Jewish law in regard to water were approved and sanctioned by our Lord when he instituted baptism by the sprinkling of water upon the head. The Romans had an annual religious feast in honour of the nymphs of the wells, when odes were sung and floral wreaths brought to garnish the waters. The feast was known as Fontinalia.

Relics of Paganism may be found in the nomenclature of wells in England, Gloucestershire having a Woden's Well, Yorkshire a Thor's Well, and so forth. Wherever the Celtic element is, there will be found the superstition concerning water leading to strange rites, and sometimes to appalling sacrifices.

The Franks offered human sacrifices to those rivers they were about to cross, and in Wales horses were annually sacrificed at St. George's Well, near Abergelen. Bulls, sheep, cats, and other animals were also offered up to pacify or please the well-gods in other places. Coins, vases, and silver spoons were frequently offered as tribute to the tutelary deities. That the waters annually required a number of victims was a fixed article of belief, and hence arose the terrible custom in some parts of never attempting to save a drowning person. The rivers Tyne, Spey, and Dee, among others, had a specific number of animal or human victims allotted to them every year, and in Orkney and Shetland the belief prevailed that unless sacrifices were made to appease the water-gods a terrible revenge would be taken upon the inhabitants. Sir Walter Scott refers to this belief in "The Pirate," when Bryce the pedlar is solemnly warned not to save a shipwrecked sailor, lest the rescued man should bring "some capital injury" upon him. To save a sinking man was, in the idea of the ancients, an act of impiety and a dangerous defiance of the will or decree of the gods.

The subject of well-worship naturally divides itself into two sections; first, the examples, and second, the origin and significance. In order the clearer to understand the latter, it is advisable to commence with typical instances of the custom as it prevails throughout Great Britain and Ireland. When we have observed the various forms of well-worship and the rites associated with it, we shall be able to draw conclusions with greater certainty, though it may here be premised that the subject is an obscure one, and has occasioned considerable difference of opinion among the students of folk-lore. I propose to allude to some of the best known holy wells in Great Britain, and to their legends and the customs connected with them, and then to proceed to the likeliest explanation of the whole matter.

Mr. Hope's summary of Holy Wells in

England, in his valuable work on that subject, is important as showing their prevalence throughout the country, no county being without examples. Yorkshire heads the list with 67; then comes Cornwall with 40; Shropshire has 36; Northumberland 35; Staffordshire 30; Cumberland 26; Derbyshire 24; Oxfordshire 19; Middlesex 16; Devonshire 14; Hampshire 11; Somerset 11; while the rest of the counties are represented by single figures. These figures, however, are comparative rather than complete.

The favourite saints (next to "Our Lady") to whom the Holy Wells are found dedicated are St. Margaret, St. Chad, St. Anne, St. Helen, St. Cuthbert, St. John, St. Peter, St. Augustine, St. Bede, and St. Hawthorn.

Like some of the incantations of old which, according to tradition, sometimes produced the results desired and sometimes had results exactly the reverse, the holy wells could injure as well as benefit the persons resorting to them. Tasso and Petrarch tell of springs whose waters caused whomsoever should drink of them to die of mad laughter. In England there were wells which cured, and wells which caused, insanity. Some added to the years of life, and some subtracted from them; some possessed the magic elixir which would prolong existence indefinitely, but alas! those wells were always inaccessible.

The holy wells of Cornwall are really a study in themselves. Their history begins with, or at all events is intimately connected with, the history of the Druids, who were strong believers in the supernatural potentiality of natural springs. Cornwall was one of the first parts of England to accept Christianity, and the missionaries found it politic not to interfere with the deep-rooted faith of the people in their sacred wells, each with a guardian spirit. But with much adroitness a patron saint was substituted for the kelpie, and small chapels or oratories were built near the sacred places. The saints whose names were given to the wells are often not of any considerable reputation out of Cornwall; to nearly all of them fantastic miracles are attributed. Divination is largely credited by means of certain rites connected with the wells, and here we may have a relic of Druidical teaching, for the Druids were strong on prophecy by means of incantations at the well-side. At Our Lady of Nant's Well the future can be made known by casting a palm cross into the water on Palm Sunday; and at the

WELL OF ST. KEYNE.

Holy Well at Gulnal the health of relatives and friends can be ascertained by the bubbling up of the water when a question is asked. Other superstitions are still more curious. By bathing in the Carn Brie Well, near Redruth, a man for ever avoided the risk of being hanged. This convenient well must have been in high favour in olden times. The drinking of the waters of the Well of St. Keyne, popularised in Southey's greatly over-rated ballad, enabled a man about to be married to be master for life over his wife— but woe to him if his wife drank first or "took a bottle to church." Other of the wells belong to the healing or medicinal class, and here we come to a mingling of fact with superstition, though we should strongly doubt the power of the waters of St. Nun's Well to cure insanity. It appears, however, that the patients were "boussed" or tossed into the cold water until "they forgot their fury." Half-drowned men might well be cured of their violence in this way; the marvel is that they remembered anything. The virtue of the well may have had less to do with the cure than the persistence of the application.

In that extremely interesting and informing volume, "Ancient and Holy Wells of Cornwall," by M. and L. Quiller-Couch, an account is given of about ninety-six holy wells in that county alone, and even that list is not supposed to be exhaustive. The late Mr. Thomas Quiller-Couch, whose notes are chiefly used in the volume, made a pilgrimage of several months' duration to the sacred springs. Some of them he found to be little more than names and traditions; others had no history, or the history was lost, but the majority were still legend-haunted, the abode of superstition, the scenes of quaint ceremonies, and connected by name with the early Christian saints. "In places the most remote and secluded," he wrote, "the old pisky tutelage of pre-historic date still clings to and protects them, and still claims to dispense the virtues of the water My humble aim is to save, within my very small tether, all that continues to us of a nearly extinct faith, its material remains, and its legendary fragments." The Cornish saints were almost wholly from Ireland and Wales, and the worship and ritual connected with the Cornish springs is almost identical with that in those two countries. No doubt the most popular, because the most singular, is the Well of St. Keyne, and the history of the pure and beautiful woman whose name it commemorates is full of charm. She hoped, as it is worded, " to benefit the world by giving to woman a chance of equality with her

MENACUDDLE WELL.

lord and master," hence the peculiar powers of the spring which she blessed, and by the side of which she died. Menacuddle Well, of which we give an illustration, belongs to a totally different class, being wholly medicinal. It is near St. Austell, and is in private grounds. The water obtained a high reputation for purity and health-giving properties, and weakly children were regularly bathed in it. The people ascribed mystical virtues to the spring, and trusted to it for the total cure of ulcers and other diseases. It was a "pin well" also, and brought good luck to those who wished as they threw crooked pins into the granite basin.

The illustration of the Well of St. Keyne and of Menacuddle Well are from the charming volume entitled "Ancient and Holy Wells of Cornwall," by M. and L. Quiller-Couch, and have been kindly lent to us by the publisher, Mr. Chas. J. Clark, 4, Lincoln's Inn Fields, London, W.C.

The Rev. R. S. Hawker's ballad of the "Doom-Well of St. Madron," tells us of a visit of King Arthur who was bidden by the monks to try the ordeal—

> "Plunge thy right hand in St. Madron's Spring,
> If true to its troth be the palm you bring;
> But if a false vigil thy fingers bear,
> Lay them the rather on the burning share."

The man of pure heart came out unscathed,

but the traitorous Mordred's hand was scalded by the furiously bubbling water when he also submitted to the test. In regard to this same well, Mr. Borlase, the great authority on all folk-lore and antiquities connected with Cornwall, says— "Here people who labour under pain, aches, and stiffness of limbs, come and wash; and many cures are said to have been performed. Hither, also, upon much less justifiable errands, come the uneasy, the impatient, and the superstitious, and by dropping pins or pebbles into the water, and by shaking the ground round the spring so as to raise bubbles from the bottom at a certain time of the year, moon, and day, endeavour to settle such doubts and injuries as will not let the idle and the anxious rest."

There is no doubt that the Pool of Bethesda, which figures so prominently in one chapter of the New Testament, was a Holy Well in the usual meaning of the term. Its virtues bore a strong resemblance to the particular curative properties of many wells in Great Britain, the waters being efficacious in diseases affecting the limbs. It may well be compared with that most famous of all the holy wells in this island, the Well of St. Winifred at Holywell.

Saint Winifred was a virgin who lived in the seventh century in a nunnery founded by her uncle, a holy man and a priest, named Beuno. She was of noble family, her father being the second man in the kingdom of North Wales. Winifred was observed by Caradoc, Prince of Wales, who was struck by her beauty, and sought her in marriage. She refused him, and he endeavoured to carry her away by force. Then, says the legend, she fled towards the church, pursued by the prince, who, in overtaking her, drew out his sabre in his rage, and struck off her head. The severed head bounded down the hill, entered the church door, and rolled to the foot of the altar where Beuno was officiating. Where the head rested a spring of uncommon size and purity burst forth ; a fragrant moss (now called St. Winifred's hair) adorned its sides, and her blood spotted the stones, which, like the flowers of Adonis, annually commemorate the facts by assuming colours unknown to them at other times. It has been discovered, however, that this moss is not peculiar to the spring at Holywell; a similar growth is found in Carnarvonshire. As for the redness of the stones at the bottom of the basin it is found to be due to a moss which

Linnæus termed *Bissus Jolithus*. It causes any substance to which it adheres to have the appearance of being smeared with blood, and if rubbed it yields a smell like violets. Linnæus believed it to be serviceable in eruptive disorders. But to return to the miracles of St. Winifred. The head was picked up by Beuno, who at once offered up prayers and intercessions for the restoration of the ill-fated virgin's life. His petitions were heard; the head joined again to the body; and St. Winifred lived fifteen years longer in the highest repute. Miracles were wrought at her tomb as well as at the sacred well.

In 1774 the following account, which I think fully deserves quotation for more than one reason, was written of the Well of St. Winifred:—
"As to the legend of St. Winifred, it is more than enough to discredit it that Giraldus, who seldom misses either a miraculous well or an extraordinary story, when they come in, should yet be silent as to both; and this, too, though he passed a night at a religious house near the place. But besides his, there is also as deep a silence amongst all our ancient historians. There is, however, a chapel dedicated to this St. Winifred, hewn out of the solid rock, and very neatly adorned,

that stands over the spring, which rises with great force, and runs afterwards with such rapidity as to turn a mill. It is from various circumstances probable that this is not so properly a fountain as a subterraneous current diverted hither by miners in working the rocky hill, and therefore Giraldus Cambrensis, though he says not one word of either saint or well, helps us to a good account of the surprising coldness of the bath by telling us a silver mine had been wrought or sought for thereabouts. Be that as it will, the name of Holy Well is ancienter than that of St. Winifred, and might very naturally induce the monks of Basingwerk, to whom by that name it had been granted, to frame the legend of Winifred and her martyrdom for that purpose. Independent of all that, it is an admirable spring, and deserves to be called the principal one of its kind." In 1784, the tourist, Pennant, found the roof of the chapel overlooking the well hung with crutches of cripples who had been cured. "In the summer," he said, "persons are to be seen in the water, in deep devotion, up to their shins for hours, sending up their prayers, or performing a number of evolutions round the polygonal well, or threading the arches a prescribed number of times."

This custom was fatal to Sir George Peckham, of whom it is recorded that in visiting the well in 1635, he "continued so long repeating his pater nosters and 'Sancta Winifreda, ora pro me,' that the cold struck into his body, and after his coming forth of that well he never spoke more." It is worth noting as a matter of history that St. Winifred's Well was visited by King James II. in 1688, and he "received for his pains the shift worn by his great-grandmother at her execution."

Of miracles wrought at the wells we have numerous traditions, and a great variety of subjects and experiences is provided. We will give some typical instances, varying from the sublime to the ridiculous, and proving that local gossip was occasionally mixed with ancient legends.

On the authority of Richard Baxter, the divine, we learn that there was a well at Oundle, in Northamptonshire, which could emit drum-like sounds when great historic events were in progress. He heard it "drum" when the Scots came into England, and was told it "drummed" again when King Charles II. died. The reason of this is hard to understand.

St. Tecla's Well, in Denbighshire, was believed

to have the special and peculiar virtue of curing epilepsy by transferring the complaint to a cock or a hen. The patient went to the well after sunset, washed himself in the well-water, and made an offering of fourpence. Then he walked three times round the well, repeating the Lord's Prayer each time. If the patient were a man, he carried a cock in his arms on these occasions; if a woman, she carried a hen. After due observance of these formalities at St. Tecla's Well, the patient went to the church, crept under the altar, used the Bible for a pillow and the communion cloth for a coverlet, and slept in the sacred place all night, keeping fast hold of the bird all the time. Next morning the patient made a further offering of sixpence, and departed, this time leaving the bird in church. If the bird died, it died of a disease which had been transferred to it; if it survived, the patient had to seek another remedy, or regard his case as hopeless.

The "Ebbing and Flowing Well," near Settle, has characteristics which must naturally have excited attention and wonderment in olden times. A rapid change in the level of the water can be observed by the visitor, and for a long period many theories were vainly advanced to account for the phenomenon. At length one, Thomas Hargreaves, constructed an imaginary model on the principle of the double syphon, and supposed to represent the syphon-like conduits of the rock. As this model imitated the action of the water it was regarded as affording the long-sought explanation. About the well a quaint legend clings, having something in common with various other legends connected with fountains, streams, and springs. A satyr pursued a lovely maiden; she, breathless and exhausted, prayed the gods to save her, and was immediately converted into the well, and the rising and falling waters represent the panting of her virtuous breast. Variations of this legend exist in great quantity.

Two hundred years ago, Dr. Knerden made record of the custom of dropping pins into wells, notably into that dedicated to St. Helen, at Brindle, in Lancashire. On August 18th, which was the Saint's day (Helen being the famous Empress who defended the persecuted Christians of Britain after her marriage with Constantine), the people assembled and cast pins into the holy water, a pin, especially a crooked one, being believed to be peculiarly acceptable to the saints, and even to the Virgin Mary. There are "Pin Wells" in many parts of England and Wales, and so great is the efficacy of the offering that those who drop the pins may wish for what they like with the certainty of having their desire gratified.

It thus became customary for the Pin Wells to be much resorted to by sighing maidens and dejected lovers, as well as by people in search of "good luck." A new superstition also arose that whenever a new pin was dropped into the well all those which had been cast in previously rose to greet it. Eye-witnesses could be produced to attest to this fact. Why saints and fairies should be so easily propitiated by so small an offering, however, is more or less a mystery. By throwing pins into the Holy Well at Rorrington, Shropshire, the villagers believed that they would enjoy good luck, and be preserved from being bewitched.

It is not only crooked pins that are in favour as offerings or as a means of divination. Occasionally the presents take a more costly form. To Saint Helen, the guardian saint of a well in Yorkshire, pieces of cloth are most acceptable. The belief prevails that weakly children can be cured of their infirmities by dipping them in St. Bede's Well, Jarrow, and meanwhile dropping crooked pins in the water. The pins were held to be equally efficacious at Sefton, in Lancashire, to test the fidelity of lovers, and at St. Dwynwen's Well, in Anglesey, to prevent love-sickness.

The hypothesis has been ingeniously set forth that the offering of pins, pebbles, twigs, and rags, was not primarily a thank-offering but an endeavour on the part of primitive man to effect a union or connection between himself, the worshipper, on one part, and the divinity or genius of the place on the other. But this seems a far-fetched theory, and an ignoring of the meaning more obvious and close at hand. Just as the warrior of old hung his buckler or casque in the temple of his gods, just as the victors in the Olympian games brought their wreaths to the sacred places, just as to-day thank-offerings are placed in the church, so in early times tributes, rich and poor, were brought to the holy wells by those who had received or still sought benefits. As for the common use of pins in these observances, it is well-known that to these simple articles a great deal of superstition has attached, and an inordinate amount of magical properties been attributed. The professor of folk-lore solves the mystery of the offering by declaring that "country girls imagine that the well is in charge of a fairy or spirit who must be propitiated by some offering, and the pin presents itself as the most ready or convenient, besides having a special suitableness as being made of metal." This cannot be taken as final. Pins were neither cheap, ready, nor convenient, centuries ago when the custom was observed. I incline to the belief that the pin-offering was originally a costly one, and that a pin-superstition led to the general adoption of the custom. In addition to all this it must be remembered that the holy wells of Great Britain may be divided into groups, and that in certain defined sections of the country observances obtain which are not met with, or only met with in isolated cases, elsewhere. The pin-wells are one separate group; garland-wells are another; rag-wells are another. A map might be drawn portioning out these districts. Then there are wishing-wells and medicinal-wells, and again we may find the two sorts fairly well grouped in different districts. Distinctive elements of worship and ritual are to be traced in these districts, and the conclusion arrived at is that though there were common influences at work, there were various origins and developments of the custom. The ultimate height of well-worship is represented in the "animal god" which Celtish imagination evolved as the animating element of the waters. "From the small beginnings," writes Mr. Laurence Gomme, "where the survival of some ancient cult is represented by the simple idea of reverence for certain wells mostly dedicated to a Christian saint, through stages where a ceremonial is faintly traced in the well-dressing with garlands, decked with flowers and ribbons; where shrubs and trees growing near the well are the recipients of offerings by devotees to the spirit of the well; where disease and sickness of all kinds are ministered to; where aid is sought against enemies; where the gift of rain is obtained; where the spirits appear in general forms as fairies, and in specific form as animal or fish, and finally, it may be, in anthropomorphic form, as Christian saints; where priestesses attend the well to preside over the ceremonies; with the several variants worshipping at every stage, and thus keeping the whole group of superstition and custom in touch one section with another; with the curious local details cropping up to illumine the atmosphere of Pagan worship, which is so evidently the basis of reverence for wells—there is every reason to identify this cult as the most widespread and the most lasting in connection with local natural objects."

From "Pin Wells" we now come to the wells at which the ceremony of "dressing" takes place. The decoration of the five wells at Tissington, near Ashborne, Derbyshire, has acquired considerable notoriety in consequence of the elaborate and imposing nature of the ceremonial. On Holy Thursday in Ascension week the whole village devotes itself to the festival. The inhabitants keep open house, and indulge in general rejoicings. Garlands of newly-gathered flowers, or boards covered with soil and fantastically arranged with floral mosaic work, are arranged about the wells; and after service at church a procession is formed, and the shrines are visited. Various sacred services are performed, the psalms for the day being read and hymns sung; then the bells are rung, and music is rendered in public by bands. The proceedings are strongly reminiscent of the Roman and Greek customs of building altars near springs, and worshipping the goddess Flora at the beginning of the month of May. There is little question of this being a genuine survival of a very ancient, and probably

Pagan, practice—one that is found in varied forms in other parts of England, as well as throughout Europe.

Well-flowering, or well-dressing, in the May-time of the year is not the least charming of

THE TOWN WELL, TISSINGTON.

the many observances or rituals connected with the sanctified waters. To visit a well at sunrise in the month of May was deemed most propitious, and neither the interdict of the Council of Tours nor the imposition of penances by King Egbert, nor the proscriptions of the early saints, nor the prohibitions of the bishop, could abolish the "heathenish practices." There is no doubt that although the Christian Church tolerated the re-dedication of the wells to the saints, it regarded well-worship with much aversion and with some dread. All authorities agree that the custom was discountenanced by the missionaries and their successors, who, however, finding it impossible to eradicate a belief so deeply rooted in the minds of the Celtish races, wisely gave to the custom of well-worship a newer and higher significance.

At Droitwich there was a salt well which was annually "dressed" on the day of the tutelary saint. One year the custom was omitted, and the spring dried up soon afterwards. The custom was revived the following year, and the water again burst forth. The righteousness of the "dressing" was thus established beyond all cavil.

St. Chad's Well, Lichfield, was named after the evangelist whose custom it was, so tradition says, to stand naked in the water and pray. The stone upon which he stood is still to be seen. The well was "dressed," and the Gospel was read to the assembled people on Ascension Day, until the beginning of the present century.

The Holy Well, near Dalston, Cumberland, was the scene of religious rites on stipulated occasions, usually Sundays. The villagers assembled and sought out the good spirit of the well, who was "supposed to teach its votaries the virtues of temperance, health, cleanliness, simplicity, and love."

There is little doubt that well-worship originally had a direct connection with sun-worship; hence arose the custom of visiting the wells for special purposes at times when the sun was rising, setting, or exactly overhead. In some cases, too, the patient had to "turn round with the sun," in order to obtain his desire from the well.

A spiritual significance also attached to some of the traditions. The man who declared that the spirit of wisdom lay at the bottom of Mimir's well no doubt knew the use of symbolism. Those who told of marvellous transformations after a visit to, and a use of, pure, stimulating, life-giving water instinctively spoke truth, even if it were cast in the form of allegory. To the soiled, the weary, the feverish, the struggling pilgrims of old, there can be no question that the wells appeared to be enchanted, and of their potentiality mysterious fables would arise.

Cursing wells, Prophetic wells, Demon wells, and wells of mysterious origin, numerous as they are, may be very briefly dealt with. I select a few examples :—

An olden records runs—" At Funthill Episcopi, higher towards Hindon (Worcestershire), water riseth and maketh a streame before a dearth of corne, that is to say, without raine, and is commonly looked upon by the neighbourhood as a certaine presage of a dearth, for example, the dearness of corne in 1678." Here we have the water, by some phenomenal means, becoming voluntarily prophetic.

The best known "Cursing well" is that of St. Elian in Denbighshire, where by casting a pin and a pebble into the water a man may cause an enemy to pine away and die. To ensure the doom falling upon the right enemy the name of the person cursed must be inscribed upon the pebble.

Leland in the sixteenth century found a strange legend attached to St. Oswald's well at Oswestry. A supernatural origin was ascribed to the waters, for it was said that when the saint was martyred an eagle snatched away one of his arms from the stake, and eventually let it fall where the spring subsequently gushed forth. This is a famous wishing well, and anyone may have his or her legitimate desire by bathing the face in the water, or casting a twig into the well.

THE HALL WELL, TISSINGTON.

St. Cuthbert's well, Bellingham, Northumberland was the scene of an extraordinary and much-famed "cure" in the twelfth century, when a foolish girl who loved frippery and fine dress was given a lesson of unusual severity. It seems that she had determined to finish making a rich and costly garment instead of going to church, when suddenly her left hand contracted "so that she could not move the fingers to open the hand, nor could those who were with her draw away by force the cloth she grasped." She was bidden to drink of the water of St. Cuthbert's well and spend a night in prayer. This injunction was obeyed, and during the night St. Cuthbert himself came and restored the girl's hand. To him, and to the water of the well, was the cure therefore attributed.

At Wavertree there is a well at the bottom of which lay, not truth, but a devil. All travellers were supposed to give alms on drinking; if they omitted to do so a sardonic laugh from the devil sounded in their ears. An inscription over the well, dated 1414, runs—"Qui non dat quod habet, Dæmon infra videt." This is improved upon in the case of a well situated between Ruckley and Acton where, according to popular belief, the devil and three of his imps are to be seen in the form of frogs.

There is (or was) a holy well in Ireland in which lay a sacred trout, and was much resorted to by reason of the marvellous cures it wrought.

At Kilmore two black fish, which never get larger or smaller, are the guardian spirits of the well. At Tober Kieran the well is inhabited by two beautiful trout. One was caught by a soldier, when it immediately turned into a woman. In awe the man loosed his hold; the woman sank back into the water, and turned into a trout again.

The Holy Well, or Blood Spring, at Glastonbury is supposed to have its source in the Chalice of the Last Supper which was buried on the hillside by Joseph of Arimathæa. The legend has been many times cast into verse, and is fit for a poet's theme. The crystal water, we are told, bubbles up incessantly, affected neither by frost nor drought, and defying man's invention to direct its course or find its origin :—

> "No hill supplies
> Its shining waters; straight from out the cup
> It springs, and shall spring ceaselessly, for aye
> A gift, a miracle, from God to man."

It is chalybeate water, and the iron in it is easily oxidised as it becomes exposed to the atmosphere. It thus leaves a red deposit on the stones it passes over and these spots are known as "blood drops," and regarded as confirmation of the legend of the origin of the spring. The water is decidedly medicinal. Mr. Hope in his exhaustive work on "The Legendary Lore of the Holy Wells of England" (1893) ascribes a two-fold origin to such legends and traditions. They are, he says, sacred and pagan—the sacred being derived from the miracles recorded in Scripture, and the Pagan being due to the primitive belief in Naturalism. As primitive man advanced in his Natural Religion he associated each specific deity with attendants, and thus around the well-gods were grouped the nymphs and naiads. The prevalence of the belief seems to be world-wide. Magic powers were invariably, and as a matter of course, attributed to medicinal wells, and their peculiar properties were regarded as the characteristics of the presiding or guardian deities.

A quaint old writer in a disquisition on the mineral springs of Great Britain, pertinently sums up the matter by showing how in process of time, religion came to have a share in remedial and beneficial usages, and "those places in which the first preachers of Christianity (who in the next age were all canonised) had commonly baptized their converts were supposed to have a certain degree of sanctity, and were from thence styled Holy Wells. The monks improved upon this, and in their fictitious legends attributed miraculous properties to certain springs, in some of which they had discovered medicinal virtues. At the Reformation, as if all things introduced or commended by the Papists were infected with Popery, the use of these wells was unaccountably run down, till man's mind being settled by degrees, reasons again recommended what had been discredited by superstition: for undoubtedly there was not less folly in refusing to make use of springs and lakes, because their virtues were attributed to false causes by Divines, than to decline their assistance because physicians disagree about their contents. The all-wise Creator has given us waters for drink and for physic, and it is an act of Religion to point out and preserve the memory of these blessings." And so forth, in the same commendable strain of common sense.

Folk-lorists can tell us of the universality of water-worship among the Celtic races, of the reasons which led them to regard wells and springs and rivers with veneration, of the Pagan rites which were afterwards adapted to Christian customs, of the direct connection between well-worship and rain-worship and sun-worship, of the inner meanings of the legends concerning wells and miraculous cures, and the survival to this day, in various forms and disguises, of the archaic creeds and ceremonials. The maiden who seeks a good husband at the well-side, the peasants who sing their songs and cast pins into the water, the mothers who dip their babes in the healing springs, the crowds who bedeck the wells with flowers, are all perpetuating the time-old superstitions of primitive man.

"What ethnography has to teach of that great element of the religion of mankind, the worship of well and lake, brook and river, is," says Dr. Tylor, "simply this—that what is poetry to us was philosophy to early man; that to his mind water acted not by laws of force, but by life and will; that the water-spirits of primeval mythology are as souls which cause the water's rush and rest, its kindness and its cruelty; that, lastly, man finds in the being which, with such power, can work him weal and woe, deities with a wider influence over his life, deities to be feared and loved, to be prayed to and praised, and propitiated with sacrificial gifts."

Well-worship has been identified with the agricultural life of aborigines who had not been able to conceive or develop higher ideas of deities.

The superstition prevailed throughout England, and in Ireland no religious place was without its holy well. As the cult is everywhere found to be prevalent, special reasons have to be sought to explain it, for no local or isolated factors will suffice. Some great dominating force must have been operative to have such wide-spread results, and we have to consider whether well-worship "originated from above and spread downwards among the people until it became universal, or whether it began from the people and penetrated upwards." We have next to discover whether it was itself a primitive creed, or the outcome of other creeds or forms of worship. It can be ascertained that it was incorporated into the Roman Catholic ritual; but on the other hand, the Saxon clergy forbade the people to continue the ancient and decidedly popular custom. Mr. Laurence Gomme thinks the facts tend to show that well-worship did not become prevalent by the agency or through the medium of the Christian Church; neither does he think it is due to the influence of Aryan culture, which received rather than generated it.

These quaint superstitions linger in rural spots; the legends are cherished, the naiads, the fauns, and the water-saints are subjects of firm faith—and on the whole we need not regret that these things are so. Few of the ancient survivals are less harmful and more poetic. The lover of romance and sentiment, and even the least susceptible to the charms of nature, will never grow weary of the creed which tells him that the sparkling waters are the haunt of laughing nymphs or listening saints, and that in the glint of streams, or the placidity of deep, cool wells may be detected the reflection of the visage of the attendant sprite. There is something too felicitous in the idea to abandon it willingly; something too alluring in the fancy to submit it to a too rigid analysis of science. A wealth of mediæval lore has gathered about the revered places where the watersprings bubble, and they preserve the names of many blessed men and women, who, by their good deeds, deserve so delightful a memorial. For ourselves we are ready to say, let benedictions still be uttered by the water's edge, let the old wells still be decked with mottoes and wreaths, let the villagers still assemble to offer alms or to receive, and even let the crooked pins still be dropped to propitiate a patron saint, or to satisfy a shy maiden's anxiety as to the devotion of her lover. These are the superstitions and observances which are rather to be encouraged than despised, for they link us with generations of the past, and in pleasant, unoffending form draw continuous attention upon those places of balm and refection which our ancestors not unfittingly deemed consecrated, and to which they therefore rendered homage or worship "simple and more dignified than a senseless crouching before idols."

Hermits and Hermit-Cells.

BY THE REV. J. HUDSON BARKER, B.A.

"MY book is the Nature of created things. In it, when I choose, I can read the words of God." Such was Antony's answer to the enquiry of the Greek philosopher or sophist who wondered how he could possibly live without books.

In that answer lies the keynote of much that seems to us inexplicable about the life of the hermits. The truest of their kind were Nature lovers. Their years were "bound each to each by natural piety."

Anchorites and hermits like Paul and Antony of the Thebaid were the Wordsworths and Austins of ancient times, who saw and understood the beauties of God in the cliffs and cascades of the wilderness and the opening buds of the garden, even though they were not, like modern poets of nature, able to impart with their pens to others the thoughts inspired by mountain, rock, and sea. There has always been a certain class of men and women who has found the essence of life's enjoyment in solitary meditation, or who has seen the highest motive of life to be the recognising of God in the works of Nature.

Quite apart from christianity the spirit of the hermit is natural to some. Even in the philosophies of Greece we find the Stoics and Cynics studiously keeping apart from their fellows lest sympathy and contact with others should be a source of contamination. The wizards and witches of the dark ages are probably lineal descendants of the recluses of some old-world religion of fairies and goblins and nature worship. No one can read Sir Edwin Arnold's "Light of Asia," without at once being reminded, in Buddha's history, of the hermits of christianity, while the fakirs of modern India prove that the spirit of the hermit is not confined to times nor limited to certain areas.

Again and again has the world at its crises had its course marvellously altered by the unveiling of one of these veiled prophets—the coming forth into the light of common day from the darkness of retirement for the stemming of warfare, for the relief of those afflicted with pestilence, or for the righting of wrongs, of some hermit who, having learned to control his own will, is fittest to control the will of others.

Then the spirit of the hermit has appeared in a new light when giving vent to all the pent-up energies acquired by years of solitary retirement and meditation, as though he would atone for his seeming want of sympathy with his fellows by a superabundant supply in emergencies. Even so in Chrysostom's early days the hermits came from their Syrian retirement and gained for Antioch pardon for the insult to the Statues. The Nitrian hermits came to nurse the plague-stricken Alexandrians, and Peter the Hermit fired the world with enthusiasm for the First Crusade.

There is something wildly fantastic and often sensationally romantic in the histories of hermits, yet beneath the sentiment and beneath the romance lies a reality—a stern reality of will's endeavour to amputate from life the worst passions of nature, and often with them those which make nature loveable. There is a forgetfulness on the part of the hermit that the parable of the tares may be applied to the microcosmos of man's own individual soul no less really than to the harvest field of God's world.

Yet the hermit life was often in earlier times possibly an absolute necessity to many who entered upon it. Even in Anselm's day the secular life, synonymous with that of sin, or the religious life of ascetic rule were the only alternatives. With all its flaws and its alienation from social life, the system of the hermit emphasised the grandest principle of the christian ethics—unselfishness—and both in the Grecian and Roman communities made practical what S. Paul himself dared not even hint at—the abolition of slavery; for it taught that there was no disgrace in manual labour, and it taught this not merely in theory but in practice, when the cultured courtiers of the Byzantine or Roman palaces retired to sow and reap on the banks of the Nile, or nurse the sick in the pestilential slums of the great cities.

The origin of the name "hermit" is interesting. Its form in the writings of Jerome and in Latin deeds of the Middle Ages show its derivation at once from ἐρῆμος—desert, for they adopted the word ἐρημίτης straight from the Greek Fathers. The hermit is essentially one who lives in the desert. Writers with a classical tinge kept the original form as late as Milton. In "Paradise Regained" we read :—

> "Thou Spirit, who led'st this glorious Eremite
> Into the desert, his victorious field."

Though Spenser his predecessor in a pretty

description of a hermitage and chapel spells the word "hermite."*

However, the Anglicised form had been used long before. In the original of Sir George Lancastre's patent from Henry Earl of Northumberland in the 23rd year of Henry VIII., of the Conygarth with the Hermitage of Warkworth, it is repeatedly called interchangeably "Armitage" or "Harmytage." In Dan Michel of Northgate's curious old "Ayenbite of Inwit," written in Kentish dialect about 1340 A.D., we come upon the word "ermitage" in the quaint parable of how the priest in the temple of Mahomet was converted into a monk of Christ, though synchronously with this Sir John Mandeville uses the other form in his "Voyage." "At the desertes of Arabye he went into a chapelle where a eremyte dwelt." By and by, in the same chatty book, the word is prefixed with the aspirate when he tells why Mahomet cursed wine. †

> "And so befelle upon a nyght, that Machomete was dronken of gode wyn, and he felle on slepe, and his men toke Machometes swerd out of his schethe whils he slepte and therewith thei slowgh this heremyte, and putten his swerd al blody in his schethe a3en. And at morwe, when he fond the heremyte ded, he was fulle sory and wroth, and wolde have don his men to deth; but thei alle with on

* Fairy Queen, Bk. vi., Canto v.
† "The Voiage and Travaile of Sir John Maundeville," ch. xii.

accord seyde that he himself had slayn him, whan he was dronken, and schewed him his swerd alle blody; and he trowed that thei hadden seyd soth. And then he cursed the wyn, and alle tho that drynken it."

In the history of Monasticism, hermits hold two distinct positions. In the first place hermits themselves gave rise originally to communities of monks. The example of one hermit drew others into the desert beside him, and so the Cœnobitic monastery became naturally evolved. In the second place, under the evolved monastic system, some continually sighed for stricter rules and more solitary meditation, and so, withdrawing from the common life of the brotherhood, took up their abode in some cell, perhaps near to the monastery. Such was the case with St. Cuthbert, who, withdrawing from the monastery of Lindisfarne, took up his abode in the cell of Farne Island.

Great master-minds, like St. Martin of Tours, have led the van by first being hermits themselves, then founding Cœnobitic monasteries have subsequently retired to some more secluded spot among the mountains, or on some almost inaccessible ocean rock. Hence it is often difficult in investigating the origin of a hermitage near unto an abbey, to decide whether the cell was established first, and then led to the formation of the neighbouring abbey, as the Cell of Godric led to the founding of Finchale, near Durham, or whether an abbey was founded first, and then cells branched off from it, for the retirement of those, who, like St. Cuthbert, wished for further seclusion, or for the missionary extension of religion in dark places. Such possibly was the cell formed at Westoe, as a branch from Jarrow, and to the self-same status probably was Jarrow itself degraded afterwards, when it became simply a subordinate cell dependent upon the Abbey of Durham.

In Mediæval England hermits seem often to have played the important part of officiating minister in places far from Abbey churches. Indeed for the matter of that, parish priests in lonely spots have in much later times really led hermit lives.

In the latter part of the twelfth century, in the time of Hugh de Baliol, of Bywell Hall, a certain hermit called Walter de Bolebec gave to the monastery of Kelso his hermitage and church of St. Mary's, in the waste and forest south of Hexham, probably at Slaley. From which we should judge that he had been the ministering spirit of the foresters, herdsmen, and moss-troopers of that region, until he founded for the Præmonstratensian canons the Abbey of St. Mary's, at Blanchland, in 1175.

Generally with the hermit's cell was a little chapel or oratory in which he could perform his own devotions, and to which he might invite the neighbouring cottagers to join him. Such seems to have been the object of the hermitage built at the end of the bridge at Stockport, in Cheshire, with its oratory of the fourteenth century.

To traverse the history of Christian hermits we must go to Eastern countries, ever the natural home of ascetism and mysticism, which are always tinged with fanaticism there, whether found in Jewish Essene or later Montanist.

The first recorded Christian hermit who prominently practised seclusion from his fellows was Paul of the Thebaid, whose life and miracles are so enthusiastically narrated by St. Jerome, the greatest advocate and promoter of asceticism, both for men and women, that the world has ever known.

Partly contemporary with Paul is Antony,

whose life, written by St. Athanasius, reads more like a romance of the Arabian nights, with the wondrous tales of demonology and animal subjection to the hermit's will. Antony, in his ruined castle by the Red Sea, thought himself the first and best of hermits when he reached the age of ninety, but it was revealed to him that there was beyond him, and better than he, a hermit whom he must visit. After marvellous adventures with hippocentaurs, fauns, and satyrs, he arrived at the cave of Paul, whom he found to be 113 years old. An inseparable friendship sprang up between these two heroes of fasting and vigil, which lasted until Antony looked upon the form of the dead Paul still kneeling in prayer in his little oratory with stiffened hands uplifted to the skies, finding him even as the servants of David Livingstone (a man of modern times, but tinged with much of the good old hermit spirit which caused him to cut himself off from the luxuries of home life, that he might further the crusade of Christianity in the desert wilds of South Africa) found their master.

The example of these hero hermits was quickly followed by numbers, until the Thebaid of Egypt and the Nitrian Desert were thickly populated with self-abnegating martyrs severing themselves from human love and human hope, as well as human sin.

The system spread rapidly into Syria, ripe ever for a revival of the Essene School, insomuch that soon it was difficult to get candidates for ordination, for the secluded life of meditation was held in higher esteem than the active missionary life of priesthood. The pages of "De Sacerdotio" show how difficult it was to uproot this doctrine even from the mind of St. Chrysostom, himself a hermit forcibly dragged to ordination and an active life.

But the growing error of the unpardonable nature of sin after baptism, caused yet more stringent application of ascetic exercises to prevent the yielding to passion, and developed that strange wild phase seen in the pillar saints, whose characteristic it was to raise themselves upon some solitary pillar many cubits high, and perhaps only three feet in diameter, and there undergo all changes of weather and all dreadful horrors, until the gruesome details make one sick to read them, and wonder that human will could so overmaster the feelings as to endure such torments voluntarily. But if the feelings were blunted and overmastered, so was the intellect; for the illusions, the visions, and even the miracles of these and other hermits are but the "frothy working of a mind diseased."

Simeon Stylites was the pioneer of these pillar saints, and received his surname from this fact. The little monologue by Lord Tennyson, called after him, gives anyone who can read between the lines a singularly vivid picture of the inner working of his soul, and the motives that led to this strange life. Simeon was imitated by very many, and the fame of his saintliness and pseudo-miracles caused a perfect forest of pillars to begin to rise throughout Syria, some of the occupants of which even outsimeoned Simeon in the tenacity of their endurance.

The spirit of the hermit passed to the Latin world, but here it received a modulation due partly to the general legal constitution of the Latin world, partly to the Augustinian Theology of the age, and the solitary hermit founded the Cœnobitic monastery, with its rules and order without the wild impetuous fanaticism and mysticism that marked the Eastern monk.

The monks of the west, in the spirit of the west, tended to the study of men and human nature, and the works of man in literature and art. Yet some there are imbued with a love of Nature in her wildness, who can meditate on God and His works better in solitude, and so we find still the hermit leaving his monastic cell, and taking up his abode in mountain cave, or on some rocky islet even in the west.

Again as in the east the Eremitic system is the

HERMITS AND HERMITAGES.

check to serfdom; side by side with the overweening Norman baron is the baronial abbot laying aside his robes of office, and passing out to the hermit life, tilling the ground, digging out his cell, and showing it is no disgrace to work, but a glory.

In England, we more frequently find instances

of the Anchorite, who has a little chamber in connection with some abbey or church, wherein he dwells. Sometimes he immures himself so that he cannot get out, and is fed through some hole in his enclosure.

The picture we give of " Hermits and Hermitages" is from a M.S. Book of Hours, executed for Richard II. (British Museum, Domitian, A. xvii., folio 4 v.). "The artist" says the Rev. Edward L. Cutts, " probably intended to represent the old hermits of the Egyptian desert, Piers Ploughman's—

> "Holy eremites
> That lived wild in woods
> With bears and lions;"

but after the custom of mediæval art, he has introduced the scenery, costume, and architecture of his own time. Erase the bears which stand for the whole tribe of outlandish beasts, and we have a very pretty bit of English mountain scenery. The stags are characteristic enough of the scenery of mediæval England. The hermitage on the right seems to be of the ruder sort, made in part of wattled work. On the left we have the more usual hermitage of stone, with the little chapel bell, in the bell-cot on the gable. The venerable old hermit, coming out of the doorway, is a charming illustration of the typical hermit, with his long beard, and his form bowed by age, leaning with one hand on his cross-staff, and carrying his rosary in the other."

The hermitage or reclusorium at Hambledon, Hants., is connected with a large thirteenth century church. Built in the angle between the tower and the west end of the south aisle, its date is probably of the fourteenth century. It consisted of two large rooms, one above the other. The upper one, of which the floor is now removed, shows a drain pipe still remaining through the wall to the exterior, and this room probably the recluse would use as his ordinary dwelling-room and kitchen. There was a door in the upper room leading by a gallery through the south aisle to the parvise of the adjacent porch, so that our friend had the use of three good-sized rooms. The original wooden door in the wall of the parvise still remains. Nothing has been ascertained as to the person for whom this hospitium was erected. He is spoken of in some old documents at Winchester as the hermit at Hambledon, but the size of the rooms points to some different manner of life to that usually followed by a recluse. He may have been the sacristan, or conductor of the church music, or in some other way devoted his time and talents to the service of the church. There is no outer door, but access was obtained from the church of which the building is now used as the vestry.

Another anchorage at Walpole St. Andrews, Norfolk, is a much smaller edifice, and seems meant as a convenient receptacle for a devotee to immure himself therein alive. This cell of a holy man was probably much resorted to by superstitious dwellers in marshland.

Against the north wall of the church of Ss. Mary and Cuthbert, at Chester-le-Street, was formerly an anchorage of four rooms. In later times this was used as the vicarage.

Similar instances are found at Durham Cathedral. Over the great north doorway, with its dragon-head knocker, was a little room, wherein stayed two monks, ever ready to go down and open the door for the refugee when he rang the knocker of sanctuary. Again between the north aisle of the choir and the Nine Altars was a grand porch called the Anchorage. "Here dwelt an anchorite, whereunto the priors very much resorted, both for the excellency of the place, as also to hear mass, standing so conveniently unto the high altar, and withal so near a neighbour to the shrine of St. Cuthbert."

There was a regular service in the Salisbury Manual for the walling in of anchorites.

Even women thus immured themselves, like those three nuns at Kingston Tarrant, in Dorsetshire, for whom the thirteenth century "Ancren Riwle" was written.

Hagioscopes in the north or south side of the chancel from little chambers behind in so many churches testify to the frequency of these immured anchorites. This, indeed, was the common form of hermit in the south and midland counties, and to this kind the darker aspects of the ascetic hermit, unhealthy Christianity, weakened intellect, and demoralised humanity, essentially belong.

The Fen district in its ancient state, provided scope for hermits of the type of Antony and Paul. There in the rich, wild, green pasturage, surrounded by marshes covered with water-lilies, and swarming with pike and perch, where the kingfishers dart and the wild ducks plunge, St. Guthlac made his hermit home in the seventh century.

He had been a warrior, but he had grown tired of slaying and sinning, and so he left his ancestral and princely home for the little green mound where he made his cell, and whereon, after fifteen years of self-abnegation, of starvation, ague, and fever had sent him to his long home, there arose the magnificent Abbey of Crowland. Over another of these fen heroes, St. Botolph, arose another shrine, and round it gathered the town which still bears his name, Botolph's town or Boston.

But it is the mountainous North, and especially the romantic crags and dells of the borderland, that in England proved the best ground for the nature-loving hermit in his purest and holiest form. All over the north country there are dotted places which still go by the name of Armitage or Hermitage, showing plainly the nature of the quondam inhabitant. Similarly in Scotland and Ireland the prefix kil, kel, or cul, shows at once the place where once upon a time there was no habitation but the "cell" of some hermit, or a group of "cells" of the ancient British form of monastery anterior to the introduction of the Benedictine rule.

There is no history that is truer than that gained from place-names.

Here is the hermitage at St. John's Lee, near Hexham, a gentleman's residence, with splendid gardens, and some of the finest beeches in England, but its name shows that this was the spot whither St. John of Beverley used to retire for weeks of meditation and devotion from the busy life of the Hexham Abbey in the seventh century. From some similar cause no doubt comes the name of the Hermitage, the residence of Sir Lindsay Wood, at Chester-le-Street.

From a hermitage in Eskdale, near Whitby, Godric, a native of Walpole in Norfolk, came to Durham, during the bishopric of Flambard (1099-1128). Acting as verger at St. Giles', and listening to the lessons of the children at the school of St. Mary-le-Bow, he learnt the psalter by heart, and once more sought retirement in a cell he constructed for himself on the north bank of the Wear, near the spot where the handsome ruins of Finchale now stand.

His biography by Reginald, dedicated to Hugh Pudsey, reminds us very much in its extravagant demonology and miracle-working, of the lives of Paul and Antony. Again we hear of the extreme steps taken for self-discipline, but a new feature is added; night after night, even in the cold winter months, St. Godric will stand up to his neck in the icy Wear all the night through, just as St. Drycthelm of Melrose did in the river Tweed in Bede's day, and as Charles Reade makes his hero do in that finest of all historical novels "The Cloister and the Hearth."

North of Durham and Finchale, just before reaching Gateshead, we come to Ayton Bank, respecting which there is a very interesting document in existence :—

"HEREMITARIUM DE EIGHTON.

"Johannes dei gra. Dunelm. Episcopus omnibus ad quos presentes literæ pervenerint salutem Sciatis quod de gratia nostra speciali concessimus Roberto Lamb, Heremitae, unam acram vasti nostri ad finem borealem villae de Eighton juxta altam viam ducentem, versus Gateshead vid. ex parte occidentali dictae viae prope rivulum descendentem de fonte vocato Scotteswell pro quadam Capella et Heremitagio per ipsum ibidem in honore S. Trinitatis edificandis, habend. et tenend. eidem Roberto ad terminum vitae suae de elemosina nostra libere et quiete ab omni servitio seculari ad serviendum Deo ibidem et orando pro nobis et pro predecessoribus ac successoribus nostris.

In cujus &c. Dat. apud Dunelm 20 die Maii Ao. Pont. Sexti Rot. Fordam Ao 6, 1387."

The life of St. Cuthbert shows him a hermit at Doil, in Scotland, in his early days, and again in his declining years on the rocky Farne Island, where the seabirds learn to love him. The miracles alleged about him and other hermits in respect to wild animals, are not hard to understand when we consider the wonderful scope they had for the practical study of Natural history, and how marvellous their knowledge would appear to the untutored visitors. But for ages the miracle-working of St. Cuthbert, and of the spirit of St. Cuthbert, was believed in by the superstitious northerners of mediæval times, and had they not proof for ocular demonstration? When the storm subsided, throughout which the ringing of St. Cuthbert's hammer had been heard, and they went upon his island, did they not pick up the beads which he had wrought? We know them to be simply the entrochi of Geology, but they did not, and so they called them Cuthbert's beads, just as they called the ammonites of Yorkshire, Hilda's petrified serpents.

Away in the bosom of the Cumbrian hills, on a little island near the centre of Derwentwater, still stand the ruins of the little chapel built over the shrine of St. Herbert, the intimate friend of St. Cuthbert. On that island St. Herbert spent his hermit life, visited occasionally by his friends (perhaps from Crosthwaite, where St. Kentigern had established his Cumbrian mission), who, starting from the little pine-clothed promontory on the eastern side of the lake, bequeathed to it the name of the "Friars' Crag." There in the scene so loved by Wordsworth, St. Herbert closed his life on the self-same day as his friend St. Cuthbert, on his rocky isle. Thus was their prayer strangely answered.

St. Cuthbert is the typical hermit of the sea. Others besides him have found in the sad sound of its waves and the ever-changing lights upon its surface, groundwork for passive contemplation and perpetual prayer. St. Brendan found it on the bosom of the ocean, seeking the land of rest, the "Promised Land." St. Regulus found it on the shores of Fife, when he landed with the relics of Scotland's patron saint, and established his hermitage on the spot where, in later years, grew the city of St. Andrews.

Coquet Isle, off Warkworth Harbour, was itself a cell of retirement, belonging to the Benedictine monks of Tynemouth.

But the mention of Warkworth brings us to the most entrancingly romantic of all the hermit stories, the pathetic tale so graphically told by Bishop Percy, in the style of the old Northumbrian Ballads.

Nowhere in the world is there a more interesting

anchorage, both for its architectural design and its origin, than Warkworth Hermitage.

There lived at Bothal Castle, about the time of Edward III., a young chieftain of the name of Sir Bertram, whose love for the heiress of the house of Widdrington was reciprocated, and moreover was approved of by the lady's parents. But before consenting to marriage she required her suitor to prove his valour, and sent him a helmet for use against the Scots. In a subsequent border raid, Sir Bertram was sorely wounded, and was carried to Wark Castle by the Tweed, to be healed. His promised bride, hurrying across the Cheviot moorlands to nurse him was captured by a Scottish nobleman who had been an unsuccessful suitor for her hand, and her attendants were killed. A week later, Sir Bertram recovering, in anxiety at no tidings reaching him from the lady, goes to her home and finds that she had set out for Wark. No trace of her whereabouts being discovered, he comes to the conclusion that some mosstroopers have carried her off. Consequently, he and his brother set out in different directions under disguise to seek her. By chance, unknown to each other, they discover her prison about the same time. The brother in highland disguise is just carrying her off to safety at night when Sir Bertram in minstrel garb comes upon them and slays his brother, and the lady, discovering the mistake too late, throws herself between them and is herself slain. Henceforward the luckless victim of these sad circumstances, having been with difficulty restrained from committing suicide in his frenzy, gave himself up to the hermit life of fasting and prayer.

His friend, Earl Percy, gave to him the sequestered spot on the north bank of the Coquet, near Warkworth, where he spent his fifty remaining years in excavating in the solid freestone rock a beautiful little Gothic chapel, which still remains, in architecture of the style of Edward III.'s time.

The little grotto contains three apartments, which have been named the chapel, the sacristy, and the antechapel. Outside of these by masonwork the hermit's (or probably his successors') dwelling-room and bed-room were built.

The chapel is still entire; the other apartments have been partly broken by the fall of rock.

The chapel is about eighteen feet long, with a width and height of about seven-and-a-half feet. At the east end, reached by two steps, is a handsome stone altar, having the upper plane edged with moulding. In the centre of the wall behind is a niche for a crucifix, with the remains of a glory. On one side of the altar is a beautiful Gothic

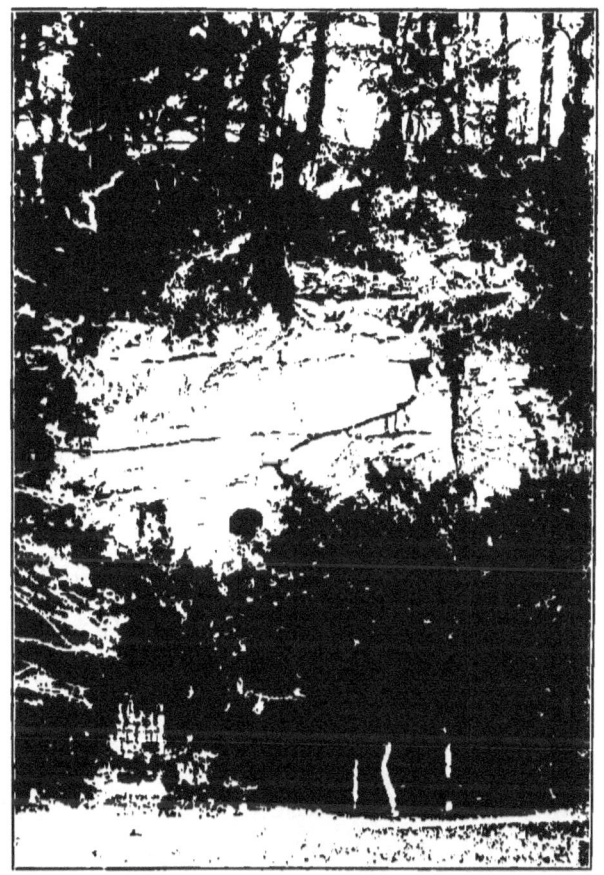

WARKWORTH HERMITAGE.

window, which admitted light to the sacristy. On the opposite side is a cenotaph bearing the recumbent effigy of a lady. Her feet rest upon the figure of a dog, as the symbol of fidelity. Beneath is the figure of a bull's head, the crest of the lady's family. Kneeling at the foot of the tomb, with his head resting on his right hand, is the figure of the hermit. A door in the chapel led to an inner apartment containing an altar like that in the chapel, and a recess in the wall for the reception of a bed, whereon one of moderate size might sleep. This then was the hermit's own sleeping apartment. Above the entrance to it is a shield, cut in the stone, and sculptured thereon are the cross, the crown, and the spear, as emblems of the Passion.

Leaving the chapel, we turn and look at the inscription, now illegible, but which once ran:—
"Fuerunt mihi lacrymae meae panes die ac nocte," and it seems like the motto not of this hermit alone but of every genuine hermit throughout Christendom; "My tears have been my meat day and night."

Outside we find the hermit's well, and a rock-hewn flight of steps to the left of the grotto, leading to the summit of the cliff, where he had his little garden, and whence he might gaze across the Vale of Coquet. This garden is now covered thick with oaks.

A series of hermits followed him in line, until

the Reformation swept away hermitages and anchorages along with the monasteries.

The last hermit at Warkworth seems to have been Sir George Lancastre, to whom was granted by the Earl of Northumberland a patent of twenty marks a year and other privileges in consideration of his daily prayers for the Earl and his ancestors in 1532. This document is still extant.

At Knaresborough, Yorkshire, still remains an interesting example of a hermitage. It is known as St. Robert's Chapel, and is hewn out of the rock, at the bottom of a cliff. We give pictures of the exterior and interior of the chapel. The chapel appears to have also been the hermit's living-room. Our illustrations are from Carter's "Ancient Architecture."

The Reformation swept away almost all vestiges of the technical religious hermit from England, but it cannot kill the spirit of the hermit. Subsequently we find it exhibiting itself in very eccentric forms in our country.

In 1696 died John Bigg, the hermit of Denton. Formerly clerk to the regicide Judge Mayne, at the Restoration he retired to a cave, and lived on charity, though he never asked for anything but leather, which he kept patching on his already overladen shoes. These remarkable shoes were preserved, one in the Ashmolean Museum, and the other at Denton Hall.

In 1863 there was living near Ashby-de-la-Zouch an eccentric character who named himself "The old Hermit of Newton Burgoland." His mania was political rather than religious. His own motto was "True hermits throughout every age have been the firm abettors of freedom," and the actions of his life were all intended to exhibit some political, social, or religious symbolism. The garments which he wore, and the plots in which his garden were laid out, all symbolised some quaint idea. Thus one hat of helmet shape represented the idea "Fight for the birthright of conscience, love, life, property, and national independence." Another of his twenty symbolic hats shaped like a beehive represented the thought "The toils of

EXTERIOR VIEW OF ST. ROBERT'S CHAPEL, KNARESBOROUGH.

industry are sweet; a wise people live at peace."

To such a weak aimless end had the hermit life decayed.

We give an illustration of the funeral of a hermit, which is one of a group in a fine picture of "St. Jerome," by Cosimo Roselli (who lived from 1439 to 1506), in the National Gallery. "It represents," says the Rev. Edward L. Cutts, in his "Scenes and Characters of the Middle Ages," "a number of hermits mourning over one of their brethren, while a priest, in the robes proper to his office, stands at the head of the bier and says prayers, and his deacon stands at the foot holding a processional cross. The contrast between the robes of the priest and those of the hermits is lost in the woodcut; in the original the priest's cope and amice are coloured red, while those of the hermits are tinted with light brown." It will be

INTERIOR VIEW OF ST. ROBERT'S CHAPEL, KNARESBOROUGH.

observed that he is to be interred without a coffin, which was customary amongst members of religious orders in bygone times.

Yet, since nothing dies, but only all things change, all that was great and good in the hermit spirit has but passed on into other forms, for still we find poets of nature and self-denying souls, and even the hermit form itself may phœnix-like arise

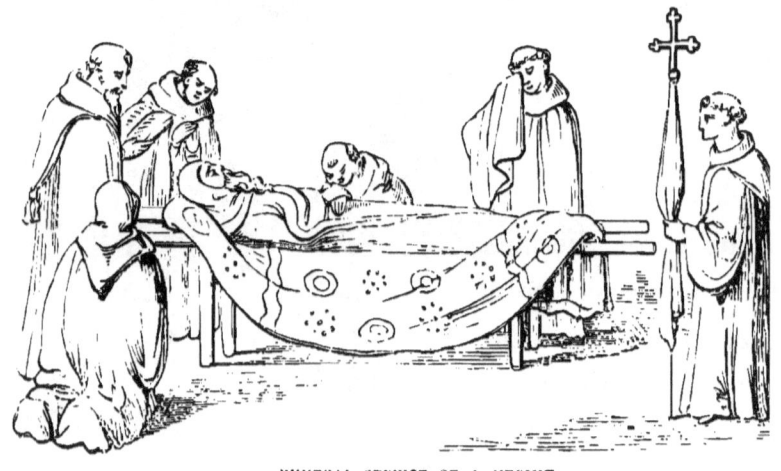

FUNERAL SERVICE OF A HERMIT.

again out of the ashes of the frivolity and secularism of the age as an overstrained reaction from the past, as it did of old. Who can tell?

It will not seem more strange to us than it did to the calm-souled fellow-christians of Paul and Antony, or the Roman contemporaries of Jerome and Eustochium.

Church Wakes.

IT is not often that we can trace back so old and wide-spread a custom as the observance of wakes to its origin. A letter from Pope Gregory to the Abbot Melito in 601, seems, however, to give us the commencement of the history of them in England. "The idol temples are not to be destroyed," he says, "but let the idols in them be destroyed. Let holy water be blessed and sprinkled in these temples; let altars be built and relics be placed there: and since they are accustomed to slay many oxen in sacrifice to demons, let them, on the anniversary of the dedication, or on the birthdays (*i.e.*, the days of the martyrdom) of the holy martyrs, construct booths around those churches which were formerly temples, and celebrate the solemnity with religious festivity." The name *wake*, in Old English *waec*, is equivalent to vigil, and arose from the custom of reckoning church festivals, from sunset to sunset, the night being largely spent in early times in watching and prayer.

The custom thus begun for religious purposes

soon developed a distinctly secular side. In the case especially of churches dedicated in the name of some more than usually popular saint the people, not only of that parish, but from all the countryside, flocked to the festival. Itinerant vendors of wares, large and small, found that the concourse gave them an excellent opportunity for trade; and those who could "turn an honest penny" by catering for the amusement of the public were not less quick in seizing the occasion.

The religious services of the festival were not forgotten or omitted, but the buisness and jollification of the time became such prominent features of the wake as to largely obscure its sacred aspect, and to call frequently for measures of restraint. So early as King Edgar's reign a Canon was enacted warning the people not to spend in drunkenness and debauchery the season specially designed for devotion and prayer. Othobon, the Papal legate, issued certain Constitutions in 1268, one of which forbade the setting out of stalls for merchandise within the walls of the Church, from which we may judge how far the business side of the wake had intruded upon the devotional. An Act of Edward I. (13, Edw. I., c. 6) goes further, by forbidding fairs and markets to be held in churchyards. In Scotland, too, measures had to be taken to secure decency of behaviour at these gatherings. The Provincial Synod enacted in 1225 that "dances and games which engender lasciviousness be not performed in churches and churchyards," and also that "wrestling matches or

A COUNTRY WAKE (WELFORD, WARWICKSHIRE).

sports be not suffered to take place there upon any of the festivals." In 1448, Henry VI. forbade any fairs to be held or merchandise to be displayed on the great festivals of the christian year.

By these means some of the more unseemly customs, which at one time accompanied the wakes, were cut off, and the sacred enclosure of the churchyard, and still more of the church itself, was defended to a great extent from profane uses; but even this was not easily achieved. So late as 1571, we find Grindal, Archbishop of York, in Injunctions issued to the laity of the Northern Province, ordering "that the minister and churchwardens shall not suffer any lords of misrule, or summer lords or ladies, or any disguised persons or others in Christmas or at May games, or any minstrels, morrice-dancers, or others, at rush-bearings, or at any other time to come unreverently into any church or chapel or churchyard, and there dance, or play any unseemly parts with scoffs, jests, wanton gestures, or ribald talk, namely in the time of divine service, or of any sermon." The conclusion of the paragraph is curiously worded, since it is obviously not intended that these things were allowable in church at other times.

The rushbearing, mentioned in this Injunction, is practically the same as the wake, the gathering and bringing of rushes wherewith to strew the floor of the churches, being one of the details preliminary to the celebration of the annual parish feast.

Kept, as far as possible, beyond the bounds of holy ground, the village carnival lived on from year to year; surrounded with much of the rough jocularity, both in word and deed, which characterized the bygone time, but nevertheless not without its pleasing features. There was much meeting of ancient gossips, many a gathering of life-long friends around the cottage hearth, or beneath the sheltering elms of God's Acre.

> "And all the village train, from labour free,
> Led up their sports beneath the spreading tree,
> While many a pastime circled in the shade,
> The young contending, while the old surveyed;
> And many a gambol frolicked o'er the ground,
> And sleights of art, and feats of strength went round."

In time, however, as "Merrie England" was changed more and more each succeeding generation into "Busy England," the multiplicity of these holidays was felt to be somewhat of a grievance, and an attempt was made to meet the case by ordering that all dedication festivals throughout the country should be celebrated on one day, namely on the first Sunday in October. This was enacted by Convocation in 1536, with the result, not that the wakes were transferred, but that many of them dropped out of observance. The village feast, however, still lives in many districts, and many fairs also keep alive the memory of the wake of earlier days; the feast-day of the patron saint of the parish, the patronal rather than the dedication festival, being the day with which they are usually connected. With the usual conservatism of the rustic mind, however, the country-folk have in many, perhaps in most instances, declined to accept the alteration of the Calendar in 1752, so that the actual observance of the Saint's Day, and the parish feast or fair, are now frequently eleven days apart.

In the old times, when travelling was difficult and expensive for the rich, and well-nigh impossible for the poor, all that the peasant or the artisan saw of life, beyond the monotonous round of his daily toil, was at the wake. "There were, at these times," as we gather from King James I.'s *Declaration concerning Lawfull Sports*, "dancing either of men or women, archery for men, leaping, vaulting, and other such harmless recreation," as well as the "carrying rushes to the church for the decoring of it, according to old customs." All such amusements Charles I., in reissuing his father's declaration, asserts to be right and proper at the feast of the "dedication of churches, commonly called wakes." But besides these, interludes, plays, and masques were performed for the entertainment of the crowd. Thomas Heywood, in an *Apology for Actors*, published in 1612, asserts that "in divers places of England there be towns that hold the privilege of their fairs and other charters by yearly stage-plays, as at Manningtree, in Suffolk, Kendall in the north, and others." In Manchester, at the wake, the pageant of Robin Hood, Maid Marion, and Friar Tuck was exhibited, and that too, it is said, within the church, the priests organizing it, and the churchwardens making themselves responsible for the expenses. Mediæval England was fond of dramatic displays. The mummers, morrice-dancers, plough-jacks, and other ministers of harmless revelry were all more or less histrionic in their performances, and pageants and miracle-plays were performed in many places with an elaboration and costliness that seem to us remarkable.

More objectionable were the cruel games too often introduced, such as bull or bear-baiting, cock-fighting, and such like; and these, in spite of the better views of our duties towards the brute creation, which unquestionably prevail to-day, lived on in some places till comparatively recent times. Bulls and bears were baited at Eccles, where was held one of the most famous wakes in the country, until the year 1834, and cock-fighting was also a popular sport there.

In recent years, with the revived regard for the Holy Days of the Church, Saints' Days are far better observed than was recently the case, and attempts have been made in several cases to emphasize the recurrence of the patronal feast-day of the parish, by organizing rural sports, cricket matches, and so on. If we can attain something of the realization of the "parochial family" once more, as it was felt at the old wakes, when old and young, rich and poor, met together for the common purpose, first of worship, and then of harmless recreation, and at the same learn by experiences to avoid the excesses of former days, we shall have done something towards the revival of Merrie England.

Fortified Church Towers.

By William Andrews.

IN these peaceful days it is not easy to fully realise the terrible times when warfare cast a gloom over the land. Our forefathers had not only to fear foes from foreign shores, but had to protect themselves against the inroads of the Scotch and Welsh.

Strong castles were conspicuous in all parts of the country. These were often the strongholds of petty tyrants and disturbers of public peace. The warlike owners of the castles with their armed retainers were often at strife with their neighbours, and even the king on the throne was defied.

Castles were not the only fortified places. Church towers, more especially in the border counties of Cumberland and Hereford, and the border districts of southern France, were strongly built, and offered a place of safety in the time of need. The best extant example in England is the tower of Great Salkeld Church, Cumberland. It has only one door, and that opens into the nave, and this is iron-plated towards the church, and at the inside are strong iron bars, when fastened, rendering it almost impossible to break through. Here the ancient town armour was kept, and here the helmet, breast-plate, etc., belonging to other days and to old-fashioned warfare, appear to be in their proper place in this ancient stronghold. At Burgh-on-the-Sands, in the same county, is an old fortified church tower. It was here that Edward I. died, on July 7th, 1307. At the time of his death he was preparing to wage war in Scotland. The church of Annan, on the Scottish side of the Solway was as strongly fortified as Burgh. This was not the only fortified church on the borders of North Britain.

Some interesting notes on this theme were written by Mr. John A. Cory, Architect, County Surveyor of Cumberland, for a meeting of the Archæological Institute of Great Britain and Ireland, held at Carlisle, in July, 1859. Respecting Newton and Arlosh church, on the coast of Cumberland, a few miles to the west of Burgh, and in the parish of Holme-Cultram, some important facts were given. "This curious example," said Mr. Cory, "is of especial interest, because the date of the construction has been

FORTIFIED CHURCH TOWERS.

ascertained. The Abbot of Holme had obtained, in 1301, a grant from the bishop, for building a church at Shenburness, at that period a place of consequence for supplies for the forces engaged against the Scots. Shortly afterwards, however, the town was destroyed by the inroads of the sea; and in 1309, John de Halaughton, bishop of Carlisle, granted licence to the abbot to build a church or chapel within the territory of Arlosh, which, subsequently to the removal of the town thither received the name of Newton, which it still bears. In consequence of the frequent hostile invasions and depredations of the Scots, to which special attention is made in the bishop's charter, the church then built was so constructed as to appear more like a fortress than an ecclesiastical structure. The doorway is only two feet seven inches wide, all the windows are more than seven feet from the ground, and not one, even in the east end of the church, measures more than one foot in width, and three feet four inches in height." The tower has in it a fire-place, and at this stronghold every precaution was made for safety in the event of protection being required. In the church tower of Burgh is a fire-place, and in other towers we have found traces of them.

According to popular tradition, the noble tower of Bedale church has proved a place of refuge when the Scotch were spreading misery with the sword in the district. It is clearly built for defence, having a portcullis at the foot of the staircase. Strange to state the portcullis was lost sight of, till it fell from the effects of a stroke of lightning. All communication with the clock bells were stopped until it was hacked away, and this was not done without considerable labour.

Another Yorkshire church tower built for defence was the one at Middleham. Richard III., Duke of Gloucester, took an interest in this church, and intended making it a collegiate church, and to endow it, but this was frustrated by his death at Bosworth. From the time of Richard III. down to 1856, the Incumbent was called a Dean, but since that year he is designated a Rector. We gather from the "History of the North Riding," published 1859, that the tower is furnished with a fire-place, constructed in comparatively modern times of Early English tombstones, etc. The Rev. Luke Cotes, Dean from 1718 to 1741, is said to have lived in this tower for some time, to avoid arrest for debt. He was involved in pecuniary em-

FORTIFIED CHURCH TOWERS.

barrassments, caused by his repewing the church, the cost of which his parishioners refused to pay.

At Melsonby, Yorkshire, is another fortified church tower. It is described as "a Norman keep in miniature." In this tower is a square aperture, said to be designed for passing in provisions to supply the garrison when located here, or perhaps for supplying a recluse, of whose habitation some traces remain.

The inhabitants of Newcastle-on-Tyne are justly proud of the elegant steeple of their Cathedral, formerly the parish church of St. Nicholas. "Other towns" says Mr. R. J. Charlton in his "Newcastle Town," "can show copies of our famous original, but all are far behind it. It is the surprise and admiration of strangers and the constant delight of the townsmen of Newcastle." In 1804, the Rev. Joseph Dacre Carlyle, the then vicar of the town, in a letter to his churchwardens said of the steeple "It is a fabric, in my opinion, the most beautiful that exists in the world—which surpasses the cathedral of St. Sophia at Constantinople, the mosque of Sultan Saladin at Jerusalem, the church of St. Peter at Rome, even the temple of Minerva at

Athens." Newcastle in the Civil Wars espoused the Royalist side, and in 1644 for ten weeks was besieged. Under the singular courage and ability of the Mayor, Sir John Marley, the town with 1500 fighting men held out against some 30,000 soldiers serving the Parliament. The Earl of Leven was enraged at being kept so long at bay by so small a force, and declared that if the town did not immediately surrender he would destroy the spire of St. Nicholas' Church. Sir John Marley was equal to the occasion and filled the lantern of the tower with Scotch prisoners. According to Bourne the old historian of the town, Sir John made reply to Earl Leven's threats by declaring "that they would upon no terms deliver up the town, but would to the last moment defend it. That the steeple of St. Nicholas was indeed a beautiful and magnificent piece of architecture, and one of the great ornaments of their town, but yet should it be blown into atoms before ransomed at such a rate. That, however, if it was to fall, it should not fall alone; that the same moment he destroyed the beautiful structure, he should bathe his hands in the blood of his countrymen, who were placed there on purpose either to preserve it from ruin or to die along with it." The spire was saved, but later, the town, after remarkable resistance was taken.

During the Civil War, Bradford, Yorkshire, was on the side of the Parliament, and when the King's troops besieged the town, the church was improvised by the inhabitants as a sort of fortress, and to protect the fabric the tower was hung round with wool-packs.

Under the shadows of the old fortified towers many tales of terror have been told of bygone times. The towers are links in the chain of history joining the peaceful present to the perilsome past.

The Knights Templars: their Churches and their Privileges.

By J. Rogers Rees.

1. THE TEMPLARS.

THE Templars, with other similiar religious Orders, were born of the Crusades. All that Christians held dear in the Holy Land was being either ruthlessly swept away or shamefully desecrated by the unbelievers, and throughout Europe a great cry went up "What can we do? What shall we give?" The Crusades were the answer; and out of the Crusades arose the mighty Order of the Red Cross Knights. It originated in the determination of two French Knights, Hugo de Payens and Godefroi de St. Omer, to devote their services to the protection of pilgrims as they travelled along the infested roads of Palestine. Seven other French Knights associated themselves in the work, and the nine accordingly pledged themselves to live without personal property, in obedience and chastity, according to the rule of the Canons Regular. Apt and expressive was

THE KNIGHTS TEMPLARS.

the title they obtained, at this time, of "Poor Soldiers of Christ;" for everything connected with them was of the utmost plainness and simplicity. Their garments were white (the distinguishing feature of the Order—the red cross—was not assumed until the time of Pope Eugenius III.); and whilst furs were forbidden them, lambs' or sheeps' skins were permitted in winter time; but whatever the dress, it was made in the simplest pattern, so that it might be put on or off with readiness. Flesh food was permitted them but three times a week, except at Christmas, Easter, and the Feast of the Virgin; whilst for bedding, a

A KNIGHT TEMPLAR.

pillow, a piece of sacking, and a single coverlet were deemed sufficient for each. Every knight was ordinarily called to attend upon the holy offices at the regular hours; if prevented he was to say thirteen *pater-nosters* for missing matins, nine for missing vespers, and seven for each of the other hours.

Their ancient badge was the Lamb: a seal attached to a charter of A.D. 1304, now in the British Museum, has the Lamb bearing the flag, with the legend around it: *Testis Agni*; but before the Templars took this device they seemed to have used that of a horse, with two men riding upon it, a rude woodcut of which is to be seen in the 1640 folio edition of Matthew Paris. Their red cross was that now known as the Maltese, with its eight points, which, as to form, was subsequently taken by the Hospitallers, who had at first used the patriarchal cross. Their banner, which they called *Beau-Seant*, was, according to Favine, "halfe white and halfe blacke, because they were, and shewed themselves wholly white and fayre towards the Christians, but blacke and terrible to them that were miscreants." What *Beau-Seant* means no one seems to be able to say with certainty; Froude thought it originated in an old cry of the Burgundian peasantry, and was originally adopted by the Knights as "a sort of link with the old home."

But the humility and poverty of the Templars appear to have been but short-lived. Bravery was an undoubted characteristic of the Order; and in those days armed force in the service of what was considered unarmed truth, was bound to be well recompensed. Accordingly, privileges and indulgences, wealth and power, were poured into the laps of the "Poor Soldiers of Christ," with the usual results. When Richard Cœur de Lion was once being preached to, and urged to give up his three favourite daughters, pride, avarice, and voluptuousness, he unhesitatingly answered that he had already bestowed pride on the Templars. Their wealth soon became enormous, and in almost every part of Europe they were found established, and in possession of churches, chapels, tithes, farms, villages, mills, rights of pasturage, of fishing, of venery, and of wood. "They had also, in many places, the right of holding annual fairs, which were managed, and the tolls received, either by some of the brethren of the nearest houses or by their *donates* and servants. The number of their preceptories was, by the most moderate computation, rated at 9,000;* and the annual income of the Order at about six millions sterling—an enormous

---

* Matthew Paris tells us their possessions included nine thousand manors and sixteen thousand lordships.

sum for those times! Masters of such a revenue, descended from the noblest houses of Christendom, uniting in their persons the most esteemed secular and religious characters, regarded as the chosen champions of Christ, and the flower of Christian knights, it was not possible for the Templars, in such lax times as the twelfth and thirteenth centuries, to escape falling into the vices of extravagant luxury and overweening pride."* William, Archbishop of Tyre, writing from Jerusalem, about the end of the twelfth century, says :—

"Quorum res adeo crevit in immensum, ut hodie, trecentos in conventu habeant equites, albis chlamydibus indutos: exeptis fratribus, quorum pene infinitus est numerus. Possessiones autem, tam ultra quam citra mare, adeo dicuntur immensas habere, ut jam non sit in orbe christiano provincia quæ prædictis fratribus suorum portionem non contulerit, et regiis opulentiis pares hodie dicuntur habere copias." †

Being so wealthy, they naturally became the bankers of those days ; and the several branches of their establishment soon became storehouses of treasure, which were faithfully preserved for, and in due course rendered back to, their rightful owners. Matthew Paris tells us that when Hubert

* *Secret Societies of the Middle Ages*, 1848 Edition, p. 252.
† *Will. Tyr.* lib. xii., cap. 7.

de Burgh, Earl of Kent, was disgraced and committed to the Tower, the King, hearing of the wealth of Hubert in the custody of the Templars, summoned to his presence the Master of the Temple, and endeavoured, by threats and otherwise, to obtain from him the aforesaid money. The refusal, however, was unmistakeable; the answer was that "money confided to them in trust they would deliver to no man without the permission of him who had intrusted it to be kept in the Temple." And so it remained until the King had extorted an assignment of it from the imprisoned Hubert, when "the king's clerks, and the treasurer acting with them, found deposited in the Temple gold and silver vases of inestimable price, and money and many precious gems, an enumeration whereof would in truth astonish the hearers." Other curious trusts were reposed in the Order. In Jerusalem, the crowns of the Latin kingdom were kept in a large chest, fastened with two locks, the keys of which were kept, one by the Grand Master of the Temple, and the other by the Grand Master of the Hospital.

Some idea of their power may be gathered from the following incident. Henry III., complaining of their wealth and pride, said to their

Grand Prior in England :—" You prelates and religious, but especially you Templars and Hospitallers, have so many liberties and charters, that your superabundant possessions fill you with pride and madness. Those things, therefore, which have been hastily and imprudently granted by our predecessors, must be prudently and deliberately recalled. I will infringe both this charter and others, which I or my predecessors have rashly granted." But mark the Templar's reply :—" It is far from thee, O King, to utter such an absurd and ungracious word. As long as thou observest justice thou art a King ; when thou infringest justice thou wilt cease to be so." Henry failed to fulfil his threat.

The wealth and pride of the Templars were the causes of their downfall in the early days of the fourteenth century. It is an interesting chapter of history, but limited space prevents our dwelling upon it at any length just here. Fuller, in his *Holy War*, quaintly puts it :—" As Naboth's vineyard was the chiefest ground of his blasphemy, and as in England, Sir John Cornwall, Lord Fanhope said merrily, not he, but his stately house at Ampthill, in Bedfordshire, was guilty of high treason, so certainly their (the Templars') wealth was the principal cause of their overthrow." He continues to say that no lives would have been taken on the Continent if their lands could have been secured otherwise, but the mischief was, the honey could not be got unless the bees were burnt, and the honey was surely sufficient to tempt rapacity. When De Molay, the last Grand Master of the Order, came to Paris, prior to his trial, he brought with him no less than twelve mules' load of gold and silver.

All the world was asked to believe that the Templars were suppressed because they were infidels and blasphemers, given to debauchery, and steeped in crime. Students, however, should give close attention to all pertinent points, and form their own judgment on the matter.

A curious sequel to the suppression of the Order is on record. When De Molay was being burnt to death in Paris, he raised his voice and summoned his persecutors to meet him straightway before the judgment-throne of God. A year and one month afterwards, the Pope was attacked by illness and quickly died. Before the same year was closed, King Philip of France died of a disease which had baffled his medical attendants, and the informant, on whose evidence the

Templars had first been arrested, was hanged for fresh crimes. Raynouard, summoning up the matter, says:—" History attests that all those who were foremost in the persecution of the Templars, came to an untimely and miserable death."

II. THEIR CHURCHES AND HOUSES.

The churches and preceptories of the Templars were not built after one uniform plan, as is sometimes supposed. They were erected to suit the exigencies of the times, the customs of the countries in which they were situated, and the geographical peculiarities of the various districts in which they lay. Preceptories were sometimes castles, sometimes ordinary manor-houses; and the churches as a rule were by no means characterised by the graceful outline and proportions of the Temple Church of the Metropolis.

In the early days of the Order, before the Templars were wealthy enough to possess buildings of their own, they used the Church of the Holy Sepulchre in Jerusalem, and from this fact some antiquaries have concluded that the round church, wherever found, is evidence of the building-hand of the Red-Cross Knights, working after the model of the church they originally worshipped in. They say:—"Wherever you find a round church, you may conclude it belonged at one time or another to the Templars." This, however, is not correct. Take, for instance, the case of one of the few round churches—that of Little Maplestead, in Essex. The whole of the parish, including the church, was given to the *Hospitallers* by Juliana, daughter of Robert Dosnel, as early as A.D. 1185, and continued in their possession until the suppression of the religious houses by Henry VIII. in the 16th century. It never belonged to the Templars.

Of course some of the circular towers and round churches were once the properties of the Red-Cross Knights.*

A KNIGHT HOSPITALLER.

The Temple in London

* "It is very doubtful whether any of the round churches in this country were originally complete rotundas. Certainly the Temple Church was not; for the oblong building on the South Side, pulled down some years ago, was undoubtedly a portion of the original design . . . and the later specimen of the kind at Maplestead had the square and the round parts built at the same time." (Cottingham, quoted in Burge's *Temple Church*, p. 14.)

was theirs, and so was the church at Acre with its round tower, "the scene of the death struggle of the band of gallant Templars who fought to the last in defence of the Christian faith in Palestine;" but we must disabuse our minds of the idea that all round churches, or rather round towers at the west ends of square churches, carry undoubted indications of their having once been in the possession of the Templars.

The Temple church in London appears to have taken upwards of fifty years in building. The circular part of it was consecrated by Heraclius, Patriarch of Jerusalem, in 1184; but the body of the church, as it now stands, was not consecrated until 1240, when King Henry III. was present at the ceremony. The feverish haste of modern contract work was unknown in those days, when men with noble ardour devoted *all*,—" money, time, thought, hope, life itself—to raise for God and man, shrines as worthy of God as human hands could raise, and fit and able to lift man's thought and hope beyond earth, and lead it on heavenward." The building has experienced many vicissitudes: in order to efface all evidence of the Popish faith the early Puritan lawyers had it well white-washed: it narrowly escaped the flames in 1666 ; was beautified in 1682, and so on. But "in the year 1706, the Church was wholly new *white-washed, gilt and painted within, and the pillars of the round tower wainscoted with a new battlement.*" The effigies were also "new cleaned and painted." This was restoration with a vengeance! In short, from the times of James and Charles I. down to the middle of the present century the Temple Church was disfigured by "incongruous innovations and modern *embellishments*, which entirely changed the ancient character and appearance of the building, and clouded and obscured its elegance and beauty." Lamenting this, a writer in the *Gentleman's Magazine* for May 1808 said: "If a day should come when pew lumber, preposterous organ-cases, and pagan altar-screens are declared to be unfashionable, no religious building, stript of such nuisances, would come more fair to the sight, or give more general satisfaction to the antiquary, then the chaste and beautiful Temple Church." The looked-for day came at length, and in the year 1840 the societies of the Inner and Middle Temple determined to give their attention to the whole matter. Galleries and screens, wainscoting, partitions and pews were thrown out, paint and white-wash scraped away; and in a little while the ancient Gothic Church of the Knights Templars "stood forth in all its native purity and simplicity, and astonished and delighted the beholder by the harmony of its proportions and its fairy-like beauty, and gracefulness of form."

We have already noticed the immense wealth of the Templars; and as a detailed enumeration of their various houses would occupy an altogether disproportionate number of our pages, we must content ourselves by pointing out to our readers where they may obtain information on the subject. A list of possessions, chiefly foreign, will be found on pp. 242-252 of *Secret Societies of the Middle Ages*, (London: Nattali, 1848); the works of Dugdale and Tanner will furnish particulars of English properties; whilst the admirable chapter on "The Rise, Extension, and Suppression of the Order of Knights Templar in Yorkshire," in Kenrick's *Papers on Archæology and History* (London: Longman, 1864), will prove of great service to those really interested in the subject. *The Knights Hospitallers in England*, issued by the Camden Society as their 1855 publication, has much information regarding the transferred Templar-possessions in the hands of the Hospitallers in 1338. Addison's *Knights Templars* (London : Longman, 1842) must also be consulted; whilst much incidental information is to be found in the pages of the several works, English and Continental, on the history of the Knights Hospitallers. It is hardly necessary to extend our list; the genuine student will soon add to it according to his own fancy or requirements.

III. THEIR PRIVILEGES.

In the year 1162, Pope Alexander III. issued his famous bull confirming the rights and privileges already enjoyed by the Templars, and granting them other and new powers and immunities. It is a somewhat lengthy document, from which we extract the following items :—

a. Permission is granted them to elect their own Master: 'No man shall be set in authority over the brethren . . . except he be of the religious and military order ; and has regularly professed your habit and fellowship ; and has been chosen by all the brethren unanimously, or, at all events by the greater part of them.'

b. They are freed from ecclesiastical interference : ' Henceforth it shall not be permitted to any ecclesiastical or secular person to infringe or diminish the customs and observances of your religion and profession . . . No ecclesiastic or secular person shall dare to exact from the Master and Brethren of the Temple, oaths, guarantees, or any such securities as are ordinarily required from the laity . . We prohibit all manner of men from exacting tithes from you, in respect of your moveables or immovables, or any of the goods and possessions appertaining unto your venerable house.'

c. But they were not only exempted from tithes: they were permitted to take them: 'As to the tithes, which by the advice and with the consent of the bishops, ye may be able by your zeal to draw out of the hands of the clergy or laity, and those which with the consent of the bishops, ye may acquire from their own clergy, we confirm to you by our apostolic authority.'

d. They are permitted to chose their own priests: 'It shall be lawful for you to admit within your fraternity, honest and godly clergymen and priests, as many as ye may conscientiously require . . . so that ye ask them from the bishop, if they come from the neighbourhood; but if, peradventure, the bishop should refuse, yet nevertheless ye have permission to receive and retain them by the authority of the holy apostolic see. . . . As regards the cure of souls, they are to occupy themselves with that business so far only as they are required. Moreover, they shall be subject to no person, power, or authority, excepting that of your own chapter. . . . It shall be lawful for you to send your clerks, when they are admitted to holy orders, for ordination, to whatever Catholic bishop you may please.'

e. Their cemeteries were to be free from the interference of the regular clergy.

f. They were to have (what soon conferred on them immense power) the privilege of causing, in times of excommunication, the churches of what towns and villages they passed through to be thrown open once a year for divine service.

It need hardly be said that such powers soon brought the Order into antagonism with the regular clergy. It was stated at a general council held at the Lateran, in 1179, that "the Templars and Hospitallers abuse the privileges granted them by the Holy See; that the chaplains and priests of their rule have caused parochial churches to be conveyed over to themselves without the ordinaries' consent; that they administer the sacraments to excommunicated persons, and bury them with all the usual ceremonies of the church: that they likewise abuse the permission granted the brethren, of having divine service said once a year in places under interdict, and that they admit seculars into their fraternity, pretending hereby to give them the same right to their privileges as if they were really professed."

The privilege of Sanctuary was thrown around their dwellings; and several papal bulls sternly forbade anyone laying hands either upon the persons or property of those flying for refuge to Temple houses.

Even the tenants of the Templars could reckon up their benefits; and in order that these might be known to all men, they erected crosses on their houses, thus proclaiming that they were free from several of the duties and services of the ordinary tenant. In the city of Leeds the cross still remains on some houses, once the property of the Templars, the inhabitants of which were free of the obligation to grind at the Soke mill.

Some of the returns made by the Templars for gifts to their Order are interesting. Camden tells us that the Templars, in gratitude for the munificent gifts of Roger de Mowbray, conferred on him and his heirs the privilege of pardoning at any time any of the brethren exposed to public penance for transgressions against the rules of the Order, provided they came and acknowledged their crime before their benefactor.

English Mediæval Pilgrimages.

By W. H. Thompson.

PILGRIMAGES amongst Christians appear to have begun about the fourth century of our era. At first the Holy Land was the destination of the faithful, but gradually other places came into vogue, notably Rome, the centre of western Christianity, and the famous shrine of St. James, of Compostella. During the latter part of the Saxon period there was quite a rage for foreign pilgrimages, especially to Rome. Hence it was Charlemagne wrote to King Offa of Mercia "concerning the strangers, who for the love of God, and the salvation of their souls, wish to repair to the threshold of the blessed apostles (*i.e.* Rome), let them travel in peace without any trouble." Again in the year 1041 King Canute made a pilgrimage to the City of the Seven Hills, and met the Emperor Conrad with other princes, from whom he obtained for all his subjects, whether merchants or pilgrims, exemption from the heavy tolls usually exacted on the journey.

The number of those, however, who could afford the leisure time and the cost, entailed by a journey to Rome, or the Spanish shrine of St. James, must have been comparatively limited. The rich of no occupation might, or the very poor who chose to abandon all lawful labour and live on charity. But to the mass of the population, such pilgrimages were impossible. Not so those to our English shrines, which later, came so much into fashion, and which were open to multitudes who could not undertake the lengthier expeditions. In popularity, first ranked that to the tomb of St. Thomas à Becket at Canterbury, popular not only in England, but all over Europe. The next in general estimation was Our Lady of Walsingham, in Norfolk. But nearly every great monastery and many a cathedral had its famous shrine, to which the faithful might resort. There was St. William at York, St John at Beverley, St Hugh at Lincoln, St. Cuthbert at Durham, St. Swithin at Winchester, St. Edmund at Bury, besides many others, where the devout might pray, and whither they might bring their offerings.

It is not surprising to us that these pilgrimages became so popular, when we learn the panacea for physical infirmities offered, and the spiritual pardons and immunities which were held out to those who undertook them. Besides, to many they were a pleasant holiday, combined with a religious function. Indeed in the course of time, the home pilgrimages generally partook largely of the holiday character. Not that for one moment we would infer there were none who took up the pilgrim staff in other than a festive spirit. Numbers there doubtless were, who, with all sincerity, thus sought to atone for an evil past, or to obtain some future blessing. Yet, with Chaucer for our authority, we venture to assert, that by the fourteenth century, whatever may have been their original intent, these shorter pilgrimages had become largely divested of any really sacred character.

We would not close our eyes to the change which has passed over our religious ideals since Chaucer's days, brought about by the Reformation and the spread of the Puritan spirit. We know well enough, how the sober and the gay, the serious and the ridiculous, were then interwoven in the national life and thought. One only needs to study the sculptures of our old churches, with their grotesque figures placed amidst the most sacred and solemn surroundings, to understand something of this incongruous mediaeval spirit. And yet after making every allowance, we maintain that in the majority of cases, eventually the pilgrimages became little more than a pleasant summer's excursion. The travellers appear to have taken every precaution to make the journey as agreeable as possible. Far from begging their bread, they put good store of money in their purses at starting, ambled on horseback in easy stages along green lanes, and lived well at comfortable inns all along the way. There was a certain costume appropriate to pilgrims, which old writers speak of as "pilgrim weeds." The especial insignia were the staff and scrip. The staff was not of an invariable shape. On a fourteenth century gravestone at Haltwhistle, in Northumberland, it is like a rather long walking-stick, with a natural knob at the top. Usually it was a staff from five to seven feet long, turned in a lathe, with one knob at the top, and

PILGRIM IN HAIR SHIRT, AND CLOAK.

another a foot lower down. Sometimes beneath the lower there was a hook or staple, to which a water-bottle or small bundle might be attached. The same kind of staff is to be found in ancient illuminated manuscripts in the hands of beggars and shepherds, as well as pilgrims. The scrip was a small bag slung at the side by a cord over the shoulder, to contain the traveller's food and necessaries. Sometimes it was made of leather, but probably the material varied according to individual taste.

Often the pilgrim is represented with the scallop shell. In an old wood-cut, illustrating Erasmus' "Praise of Folly," he appears with it attached to his hat. The

PILGRIM (*from* "*Praise of Folly*").

scallop shell had, however, more especial reference to the shrine of St. James of Compostella, being the badge of that particular Spanish saint. Sir Walter Raleigh makes reference to it, in his well-known lines:—

"Give me my scallop shell of quiet,
My staff of faith to walk upon,

> My scrip of joy, immortal diet,
> My bottle of salvacion;
> My gown of glory, hope's true gauge,
> And thus I'll take my pilgrimage;
> Whilst my soul like quiet palmer,
> Travels to the Land of Heaven."

Though, however, the conventional pilgrim as a rule, is represented with robe, hat, staff, and scrip, it is by no means clear, that the actual pilgrim always bore them. Chaucer, who gives the most minute details as to the costume of the characters in his Canterbury Tales, does not, so far as we remember, mention any of these things.

The Knight
> "Of fustian wore a jupon" (guernsey).

The squire
> "Short was his gowne, with sleeves long and wide."

The Yeoman
> "Was clad in coat and hood of greene."

The Merchant was in motley:
> "And on his head a Flander's beaver hat."

The only one of Chaucer's pilgrims, who bore anything of religious insignia, was the Pardoner:
> "A vernicle had he sewed in his cap."

The vernicle—the kerchief of St. Veronica—on the original of which the sacred countenance was said to have been miraculously imprinted by Our

ENGLISH MEDIÆVAL PILGRIMAGES.

Lord as He trod the Via Dolorosa, was borne by those who had made a pilgrimage to Rome; and the Pardoner, the poet tells us:—

"Straight was comen from the court of Rome."

The chief sign of the Canterbury pilgrims was the ampulla (a flask). The legend was that the monks carefully collected from the pavement the blood of the blessed St. Thomas, and that it was preserved as a sacred relic. A lady visiting the shrine, begged for a drop of the precious fluid, and this being used as a medicine, worked a wonderful cure. Naturally the tidings of the miracle became noised abroad,

THE CANTERBURY AMPULLA.

and as time went on, the pilgrims were not satisfied unless they too shared the same benefit. A drop of the blood was mixed with a chalice full of water, so as not to offend the senses. According to the monkish writer, who records many of the miracles, it wrought extraordinary cures. Vast crowds came to partake of the strange medicine, and those who came were also anxious that their friends at home should in turn share the privilege. At first the liquid was placed in wooden vessels, but these were split by it, and many fragments of the broken vessels were hung about the martyr's tomb. At length the thought came into the head of a certain young man to make little flasks (ampullae) of lead and pewter. And, wonderful to relate, the miracle of the breaking ceased. Then was it known that it was in these vessels the fluid was designed to be carried. Some of these curious relics still exists. There is an example preserved in the museum at York. The principal figure is a somewhat stern representation of the saint; above is a crude illustration of the shrine, and round the margin a rhyming legend:—" Optimus egrorum, medicus fit Thoma bonorum," which is thus translated " Thomas is the best physican for the pious sick."

Second only in importance to the shrine of St. Thomas at Canterbury, was that of Our Lady of Walsingham. Pilgrims flocked to it from all parts of England, and even from abroad. No less than five English kings paid their devotions in person there. For hundreds of years an excellent road, or pilgrim's way, was maintained through the East Anglian counties leading to the spot. Thither came the critical Erasmus, and he has left some of his impressions on record. Half serious, half sceptical, it is not easy to know exactly in what light the keen scholar regarded all the reputed wonders of the place. Of the scholarship of the monks he had no exalted opinion, for he tells us that in his time they did not know Greek from Hebrew. Erasmus describes the holy places, the various chapels and sights. For besides the venerated image of Our Lady, Walsingham contained many celebrated relics, such as the Virgin's milk, and a finger-joint of St. Peter. In one of his colloquies he writes :—" Presently a man's finger is exhibited to us, the largest of three; I kiss it, and then I ask whose relics were these? He says, St. Peter's. The Apostle? I ask. He said yes. Then observing the size of the joint, which might have been that of a giant, I remarked that St. Peter must have been a man of very large size. At this one of my companions burst into a laugh, which I certainly took ill, for if he had been quiet, the attendant would have shewn us all the relics. However we pacified him by offering a few pence."

Of the northern pilgrimages, one of the most famous was that to the shrine of John of Beverley, the Anglo-Saxon saint. It had many notable visitors in its day; amongst others Henry the Fifth, who came thither after the Battle of Agincourt. The reason for the journey was a story noised abroad at the time, to the effect that the shrine of St. John on the day of the great conflict, had exuded blood. Whether the King believed the legend or not, we cannot decide, but he was a good Catholic, and so we may assume he probably accepted it in good faith. Anyhow the following year he made a pilgrimage to Beverley in commemoration of the great victory which the English arms had achieved, and we trow left the minster considerably richer for his visit and offerings.

The custom was for pilgrims to travel to their destined shrines in companies. Of such a party Chaucer has left us an inimitable picture in the Canterbury Tales. They appear to have done their best to make the road agreeable to one another. Chaucer make mine host of the Tabard say :—

"Ye go to Canterbury—God you speed,
The blissful martyr quit you your mede;

ENGLISH MEDIÆVAL PILGRIMAGES.

> And well I wot as ye go by the way,
> Ye shapen you to talken and to play,
> For truly comfort and worth is none,
> To riden by the way dumb as a stone."

Each pilgrimage, we are told, had its gathering cry. This cry, in the early morning, the pilgrims shouted as they left the town, or villages, where

THE CANTERBURY PILGRIMS.

they slept overnight. It acted as a muster call for the pilgrims who were bound to the same shrine. The common custom was, for the party to hire a few singers and musicians, to enliven the journey. Before reaching a town they used to draw themselves into procession, and then, with music, to pass through the streets. The songs which the pilgrims sang, whilst on their journey, strictly should have been of a sacred character, as should also the stories that were recited, but frequently, they were very much otherwise. The songs were often love songs, and though Chaucer's "poor parson" preached a sermon, the majority of the stories told on such a pilgrimage, were probably of a light, or even loose, description. The following picture, from Foxe's "Acts and Monuments," if not very friendly, is certainly amusing.

"When diverse men and women will go thus after their own willes, and finding out one pilgrimage, they will order with them before, to have with them both men and women, that can well synge wanton songs; and some other pilgrims will have with them bagge-pipes, so that every towne they come throwe, what with the noise of their singing, and with the sound of their pipyng, and with the jingling of their Canterbury bells, and with the barking out of dogges after them, they make more noise than if the Kinge came there away, with all his clarions, and many other minstrelles. And if these men and women be a moneth on their pilgrimage, many of them shall be a half year after great janglers, tale-bearers, and liars."

We must take such a statement as this with considerable reservation. There doubtless was an admixture of good and evil, for the reader will perceive by this time, that the mediæval pilgrimage was practically equivalent to the modern tour. To refer for a while to the longer religious journeys; such as those to the Holy Land, or the shrine of St. James of Compostella, it is strange how like the personally conducted tours of the nineteenth century, were these pilgrimages in later pre-Reformation times. The "personally conducted" was quite an extensive business. The "patronus," as the conductor was called, chartered a ship, provisioned it, and conducted the pilgrims from the place of embarkation and back, at so much per head; feeding them by the way, arranging for their safe conduct, leading them in a body to the various shrines, and pointing out the different objects of interest and devotion on the journey. An English traveller in the fifteenth century counted eighty such pilgrim vessels lying at once in the harbour of Corunna, thirty-two of them English.

One of the books which Caxton printed was "Informacion for Pylgrmes into the Holy Londe," a sort of fifteenth century Murray, or Baedecker. This curious work serves to shew that really the gulf between the mediæval pilgrim and the nineteenth century tourist was by no means so wide as some people might be led to suppose. The passenger, for instance, was to look well after his berth on board, and see that he did his utmost to minimise the troubles of sea-sickness. "In a ship or caryk, choose you a chamber as nigh the middes of the ship, as ye may. For there is least rolling or tumbling, to keep your brain or stomach in temper."

He was also to take care the "patronus" did not get to the windward of him in the victualling.

"Also see that the sayd patron geve you every day hote mete twyse at two meeles. The forenoon at dyner, and the afternoon at supper. And that the wyne that ye shall drynke be good, and the water fresshe and not stinkyng, yf ye come to have better. And also the byscute."

He was counselled to provide himself with a few extras. He was advised to take some wine of his own, and half-a-dozen hens or chickens, besides various other things.

"Also I counsell you to have wyth you out of Venyse (that is, to purchase whilst at Venice) confections, comfortatives, grene gynger, almondes, ryce, fygges, reysons, grete and smalle, which shall doo you grete ease by the waye. And pepyr, saffron, cloves and mace a few, as ye thynke need. And loaf sugar also."

"Also take wyth you a lytell caudron, a fryenge panne, dysshes, platers, sawcers of tree, cuppes of glasse, a grater for brede, and such necessaryes." Evidently it was not intended the pilgrims should journey fasting, eating sparingly of the coarsest food, drinking nothing but water, travelling in rags, or with peas in their shoes.

Caxton's "Information" is severely practical and scrupulously minute. Fourteen days in the Holy Land was the time stipulated for in the covenant with the patron. It was reckoned that all the most important places could be "done" in that time, allowing four days for the journey from Jaffa to Jerusalem and back. "*Ten Days at Jerusalem,*" would have been the modern advertisement. The fees for admittance to the various spots, to be visited en route, are clearly stated in this pilgrim's vade mecum. When these directions are read, it is not so difficult to understand how

Chaucer's Wife of Bath, besides making several minor tours, had been three times to Jerusalem. Furthermore we are enabled to more thoroughly see the reason why these pilgrimages were so popular. They had their supposed spiritual benefits, but in addition to these, and the pleasure of beholding the wonders of strange countries, the traveller enjoyed several useful temporal advantages. If he were a priest, he drew his stipend all the time he was away, provided his absence did not exceed three years. If a layman, he was exempted from all taxes and public burdens. Once the cross was sewed upon his shoulder, and he had received the blessing of the church, no one could sue him for debt in any temporal court, for he was under the especial protection of S. Peter and the Pope. It thus came to pass that fraudulent bankrupts were often found in the company of those who proceeded on pilgrimage to the Holy Land.

Pilgrims' Signs.

By the Rev. Geo. S. Tyack, b.a.

THE idea of pilgrimage, the making of journeys to spots consecrated by the lives and deaths of holy persons, seems to appeal to a sentiment common to the hearts of men. Herodotus tells us of an annual pilgrimage which took place in ancient Egypt. The Semitic races, with the exception of the Hebrews, journeyed yearly to Aphaca and to Hierapolis in Syria, in honour of Astarte; and the Jews by divine command thrice every year went up to Jerusalem to keep the great festivals of their faith. The practice exists at the present time more commonly among the Mohammedans and the Buddhists than elsewhere, the former congregating yearly at Mecca in numbers sometimes amounting to eighty thousand persons, and the latter at Kandy and Adam's Peak, in Ceylon. The devotees of Brahminism also have their pilgrimages to Orissa.

Amongst Christian nations pilgrimages have been but seldom undertaken, at any rate on a large scale, in modern times, although the alleged appearance of our Lady at Lourdes, and the miraculous cures affected there in consequence, have to some extent revived their popularity in some parts of Latin Christendom. Of the prominence given to these acts of devotion in Mediæval Europe, it is scarcely needful to speak; two facts, which illustrate it, are known unto all men, namely that the pilgrimages to the Holy Sepulchre led to the epoch-making wars of the Crusades, and that those to the shrine of St. Thomas of Canterbury gave us our first great English poem.

Those, however, were only two out of many places which attracted pilgrims in the middle ages in greater or less numbers. The tomb of St. James at Compostella in Spain was one of the most famous shrines in Europe, next to which in popularity probably came that of St. Martin at Tours in France. Most countries had one or more spots well known as the resort of pilgrims. In Italy the tombs of St. Peter and St. Paul at Rome, and the Holy House at Loretto, attracted a crowd of travellers from all parts of the west. Switzerland saw them wending their way to Einsiedeln, Austria to Mariazell, France to St. Denis, and Scotland to St. Andrews. England also had many celebrated shrines besides that of St. Thomas à Becket; and Westminster, Hereford, Peterborough, St. Alban's, St. David's and other cities were all visited by companies of pilgrims anxious to pay their devotions at the holy places which they contained.

We are at present concerned with the badges or signs which were to be bought at most of the chief resorts of pilgrims, and which the purchaser wore sewn on his cloak or in his hat, as a proof that he had fulfilled his vow, or performed his penance by the pilgrimage.

These signs consisted of plates or brooches, generally of lead or pewter, stamped with some design appropriate to the place of their origin. The pilgrim returning from Rome carried a little medal graven with the Cross-keys; he from Mount Sinai bore on his cloak the wheel of St. Catherine; but the man who had visited the holy places of Jerusalem placed in his hat, or bound to his staff, two small palm-branches, whence he was known as a *palmer*, while a cockle-shell denoted one who had been to Compostella.

Numbers of metal brooches bearing the effigies of popular Saints, and once used as pilgrims' signs have been found in various parts of Europe, and no doubt the sale of them formed at times no inconsiderable source of revenue to the churches containing the shrines. It would appear, in fact, that the clergy were protected by the civil authorities in the monopoly of their production. Leaden images of the Blessed Virgin were issued as signs of a completed pilgrimage to the Church of St. Mary Magdalene and St. Maximin, in Provence: and in 1354 a Royal ordinance was promulgated by the sovereigns of Sicily, Louis and Johanna, forbidding their manufacture outside the convent. Another variety of the sign issued at this place, has the figure of St. Mary Magdalene, accompanied by her traditional emblem, the box of precious ointment, kneeling at the Saviour's feet. The arms of Anjou and Provence and a Latin inscription indicate the place of issue.

The cathedral of Amiens claims that to it was translated in 1206 the head of St. John Baptist. The relic was preserved on a great gold dish a foot in diameter, adorned with precious stones; and it speedily became an object of veneration throughout the surrounding districts. The pilgrim's sign commemorating a visit to this head, is a circular medal or brooch, on which is rudely depicted a priest bearing the head, while an acolyte with a taper stands on either side. Around the edge runs the legend :—" HIC EST SIGNUM FACIEI BEATI JOHANNIS BAPTISTE AMI" (this is the sign of the face of Blessed John Baptist of Amiens). Other signs from places where relics of the same saint were said to have been preserved have been found. In one the face of St. John fills the whole medal, another (discovered at Canterbury) has a full-length figure holding the lamb, or Agnus Dei.

Among English saints none gained so

PILGRIMS' SIGN, FROM THE CATHEDRAL OF AMIENS.

much popular favour as St. Thomas of Canterbury, and several signs used by Canterbury pilgrims have come to light. One is in the form of an effigy of the Archbishop in episcopal vestments, and with the right hand raised in benediction, riding upon a horse. Another, somewhat similar, represents him carrying the processional cross, the mark of his ecclesiastical dignity, while an attendant leads the horse. A sign of quite a different type consists simply of the bust of the martyr, episcopally vested, with the name beneath.

For the benefit, no doubt, of poorer pilgrims, smaller and simpler devices were also adopted. We find little circular brooches merely stamped with a "T," or with a head wearing a mitre, or a head distinguished by the emblem of St. Thomas, a sword. Another circular sign has again the head surrounded by the legend CAPUT THOME. Amongst these cheaper tokens is one with a pin behind for affixing it to the cap; this one is a small effigy of the Archbishop in full canonicals, bearing his crosier in the left hand, and raising the right in benediction. A more ornate specimen is oval, having the figure of St. Thomas seated, and holding his archiepiscopal cross. Pilgrims to Canterbury are said, not only

PILGRIMS' SIGN FROM CANTERBURY.

to have themselves worn badges such as these, but also to have put small bells on the harness of their horses. These had running as a legend round the rim, the words "CAMPANA THOME," and no doubt they suggested the popular name of the flower, known as the Canterbury bell.

It has been suggested that the signs which consist only of the head of St. Thomas are

PILGRIMS' SIGNS, FROM BURY ST. EDMUNDS.

probably commemorations of a visit to that part of the Cathedral of Canterbury where the head alone had its shrine, separate from that in which lay the body.

St. Edmund, "king, virgin, and martyr," was long one of the most popular of English saints. His relics were enshrined at Bury St.

Edmund's, and his sign was a crowned head in an ornamental border. Another sign emanating from this abbey was made on the model of the silver pennies and groats of the time, and bore on the obverse the head of St. Nicholas, and on the reverse a cross with the opening words of a hymn to St. Edmund. The reputation of St. Edward the Confessor was more widely spread and more enduring. A sign not unlike a modern breastpin was sold to Westminster pilgrims, consisting of a king's face, with a pin for fastening it. King Henry VI., whose unfortunate career, and mysterious death, stirred up on his behalf a share of public sympathy, gained for a short time a sort of pseudo-canonization at Windsor, and it was even asserted that miracles were wrought at his tomb. Pilgrimages accordingly took place thither, and an appropriate sign was struck, the figure of a king, crowned, and holding in either hand the orb and the sceptre, while a stag crouches at his feet.

The popular shrine of Our Lady of Walsingham issued figures of the Madonna and the Holy Child, or of small ampullae, or vases, stamped with a crowned W.

Other signs which may be mentioned are the

figure of a mitred abbot, and the name ST.
LENNARD, probably from St. Leonard's Priory,
York; a royal head with the name KENELM, from
the shrine of St. Kenelm, king and martyr, at
Winchcombe, Gloucestershire; a brooch with
figures of St. Fiacre, his sister Syra, and St.
Faro of Meaux, from the shrine of the first-named
saint near Paris; St. Eloi working at his anvil,
while a horse stands by, from
Noyon. Signs have also been
found of the Three Kings of
Cologne (a star), of St. Nicholas,
of St. Laurence, of St. Olaf of
Denmark, of our Lady of
Bologne, and of St. Christopher,
as well as others with a crucifix
upon them.

Several signs have been found
of doubtful origin, the one here
engraved being an example. It is the full-length
figure of a bishop, in full eucharistic vestments,
standing in the act of benediction, while below is
the word "*Fordom.*" Some have thought it a
sign of St. Leonard, owing to the manacle on his
right arm; others deem it a figure of John de
Fordham, Bishop of Durham from 1382 to 1388,

and subsequently of Ely, where he was interred. Offerings are said to have been made at his tomb there. It is, however, suggested that *fordom*, or "for-doom" may mean "false judgment," and refer to something in the life of an unrecognized saint.

Pilgrimage to some of these shrines was rewarded with special privileges, and the pilgrims thereto were regarded with peculiar reverence, much as a Mohammedan whose green turban announces the accomplishment of the journey to Mecca, is regarded by his less fortunate fellows. There are stories of prisoners, during the times of the long wars between France and England, having been released on their captors noticing that they wore the pilgrims' sign of Our Lady of Roc-Amadour, in Quercy. This was a medal having the Blessed Virgin enthroned on the obverse, and St. Amadour on the reverse. The shrine of St. James of Compostella, in Spain, was brought into special eminence by the fact that the Spaniards were forbidden to join in the Crusades, so long as they had not succeeded in fully exterminating the Moorish infidels from their own country; and in those circumstances a journey to Compostella was accounted an equivalent to one to the Holy City. The shell, which formed the usual sign of this pilgrimage, was sometimes reproduced in metal, and occasionally had a figure of St. James upon it. The effigy of the Saint alone was also in use.

When so much honour accrued to the wearers of these badges, it is not surprising to find evidence that some people were not unwilling to gain the reputation of pilgrims without the danger and toil of the pilgrimage. We find, therefore, no less than three Popes, in three different centuries, namely, Alexander II. (1061-1073), Gregory IX. (1227-1241), and Clement V. (1305-1314), issuing bulls empowering the Archbishop of Compostella to excommunicate anyone who sold signs of St. James at other places than within that city.

The literature of the Middle Ages has many allusions to the use of these pilgrims' signs. The supplement to the *Canterbury Tales*—which is but little later in date than the famous Tales themselves—tells us how, after venerating the holy relics shown to them, the pilgrims—

> "Then, as manere and custom is, signes there they bought,
> For men of contre should know whome they had sought.
> Eche man set his silver in such thing as they liked,
> And in the meen while the miller had y-piked
> His bosom ful of signys of Canterbury brochis."

In the Vision of Piers Ploughman, a pilgrim is described as having visited all the noted places of pilgrimage, and as wearing the marks which proved his wanderings. He had "seten on his hatte," or on his cloak, the "Signes of Synay," the "Shells of Galice," the "Keyes of Rome.

Giraldus Cambrensis tells us that after passing through Canterbury on his way to London, he wore the signs of St. Thomas hanging about his neck, and Erasmus, in a colloquy on "Pilgrimage for Religion's Sake," makes one of his characters ask—"But what kind of apparel is that which thou hast on? Thou art beset with semi-circular shells, art covered on every side with images of tin and lead." To which the reply is, "I visited St. James of Compostella, and returning I visited the Virgin beyond the sea, who is very famous among the English."

Louis XI., King of France, was greatly given to the wearing of these leaden signs, a fact to which, it will be recalled, Sir Walter Scott makes frequent allusion in "Quentin Durward."

By a transition, natural enough to frail human nature, these signs, from being merely records of a meritorious act completed, came to be looked upon as charms, as if through them some part of the blessing was continued to the wearer, which the pilgrimage was supposed originally to have procured.

As works of art these signs are for the most as worthless as they are in intrinsic value, but as surviving relics of a custom now scarcely known in England, and as illustrations of such early writers as Chaucer and others, they are full of interest.

Human Skin on Church Doors.

By the Rev. Geo. S. Tyack, b.a.

THOSE were wild and stormy days for England when the Black Raven of the marauding Dane hovered on her eastern coast, and ever and anon swooped with relentless talons on the devoted land. Time had been when the English themselves had in a similar manner harried and harassed the British who held these lands before them, but with the change of the times, their character had changed also. The sons of the White Horse and descendants of the hardy Norsemen had become tillers of the soil, and patient toilers in life's ways: while they feared no more the thunder of Thor's hammer, nor gloried in the fierce fame of fight that Odin loved, for they had knelt to the White Christ, and called themselves His men.

Yet how hardly can a man, or even a race of men become wholly emancipated from the failings of their former selves! How, under terrible provocation, the fierce nature of the wild Viking showed itself through the civilised and Christianised Englishman, this page of history shows. For up and down the country in places mostly near the east coast, but one at least, nearer the west, the gruesome legend runs, that stung to ungovernable rage by the continuous assaults of the Danes, in whose pathway farmstead, and village, and abbey, went up in flames, and specially horrified at the way in which shrine and priest were desecrated and slain, the English took once and again an awful vengeance on their ruthless enemies. As the farmer nails the rook to his barn door for a warning to all the tribe, so the maddened English seized the poor wretch who had fallen into their hands, stripped from his quivering limbs his skin, and nailed it on the door of the church which he had sacrilegiously violated.

A legend of such brutality, one would gladly dismiss as too horrible to be true, but the story rests on more than a legendary foundation.

There are at least six places in England where the church doors have been overlaid with human hide. These are Hadstock, Copford, and Castle Hedingham, in Essex; the cathedrals of Rochester and of Worcester; and Westminster

Abbey. Fragments of the skins have been taken from all these doors, except those of Castle Hedingham and Rochester, and have been submitted to microscopical examination by experts, who have in each case declared that it was unquestionably human skin. For the other two cases tradition only exists. Beneath the iron scroll-work on the Norman doors of the parish church of Castle Hedingham leather, like parchment in appearance, has been found, and the local legend says it is the skin of a man. The writer of this article is not aware that it has ever been thoroughly examined. The only allusion to the matter with respect to Rochester seems to be an entry in the diary of Samuel Pepys. Under April 10th, 1661, he writes, "Then to Rochester, and there saw the Cathedrall, which is now fitting for use, and the organ there a-tuning. Then away thence, observing the great doors of the church, as they say covered with the skins of the Danes." It is strange that a tradition of that kind, rife only two hundred years since, should now have entirely died out. Yet such is the case, and only the proverbial curiosity of Pepys in noting the smallest details that came under his notice, makes the story worthy of record and regard.

HUMAN SKIN ON CHURCH DOORS.

We have then six of these gruesome instances, four of which are fully substantiated. Legend describes the skins at Worcester, Hadstock, and Copford, as those of Danes; and the microscope has shewn that in each case it once belonged to a fair-haired man, such as the Northmen were. The hide at Castle Hedingham is said to be that "of a foreign robber," who attempted to sack the church; which probably is another slightly less precise version of the same story. The Westminster case must be treated separately, as it will occur to everyone that no hostile Danes have harried us since S. Edward the Confessor reared his glorious abbey.

This much we know for certain concerning the Danish incursions, that their ships came frequently to the Eastern coast of the country, and that Essex, as well as the neighbouring counties, suffered from their attacks, and, moreover, they occasionally ventured down the channel, and assailed the west coast also, and ran up the Severn, not only as far as Worcester, but even further.

The most complete form of the story is the one extant at Worcester. It relates that the Danes, having landed near the city, from which most of the peaceful burghers had fled on their approach, looted the houses and the great church, and then made off to their long ships. The heavy sanctus bell of the cathedral, abandoned, one may suppose, by the rest of the marauders as too cumbersome to carry off, seemed to one man a desirable acquisition, and he lingered behind his comrades to get it. Presently, before he was able, loaded as he was, to join the retreating Danes, the townsmen returned. Doubtless from a distance they had been witnesses of many outrages, and right and left along their streets they now saw signs of the violence of their foes; and in the heat of their rage and indignation they came upon the sacrilegious wretch upon whose shoulder was the sanctus bell.

We will not try to picture the final scene; the Englishmen's blood was up, the Dane was caught redhanded in theft and sacrilege, and moreover there was probably not a man in all the throng who did not burn under a sense of some private wrong inflicted on him by the pirates. Upon the devoted head of the one the misdeeds of all were visited; and his skin, in attestation of his guilt and of his doom, was fastened to the church door.

HUMAN SKIN ON CHURCH DOORS.

Such is the story which is told with more or less fullness in every instance; it is always a Dane who suffers, and always for a robbery of the Church. An old rector of Copford, in writing some "Church Notes," says that such a story was told to him concerning Copford Church in the year 1690, and that his informant, an aged man, had heard it when he was a boy.

It is not an unusual occurrence for a tradition, springing, it may be, from a historical foundation in one district, to get transferred in some way to others with which it has no real connection. But we are debarred from thinking that all these stories have sprung from one original, by the fact of the presence of the skin in each instance. No skin now remains upon the Copford door, the last vestiges having been removed about the year 1843 or 1844; a new door was also erected in 1846 at Hadstock, to which the fragments of skin that still adhered to the old one were not transferred. The great door of Worcester Cathedral was also long since removed, but it is still preserved, and portions of the human hide may yet be seen. Fragments from Worcester, Hadstock, and Copford are also preserved in the Museum of the Royal College of Surgeons, Lincoln's Inn;

and other authenticated pieces are in the hands of public or private collectors of antiquities.

A difficulty in accepting the legend in all its details arises from the computed age of the door in some of these instances. Some hold that the old doors of Worcester date back no earlier than the fourteenth century; others, however, assign them to the Norman, or even to the Saxon period. Since they are evidently very ancient, and show signs of having been altered since they were first made, they may perhaps date from the Saxon time, but have been fitted afresh to new requirements, arising from Cathedral alterations in a later century.

Another detail is affected by the fact that the introduction of the use of a sanctus bell is attributed to William of Paris in 1097, or to Cardinal Guido in 1200.

Whether the special act of sacrilege was the theft of a sanctus bell, or of some other article of church furniture; whether the robber were Saxon, Norman, or Dane; the presence of the human hide is a witness for the truthfulness of the most terrible part of the story.

The skin found on the doors at Westminster Abbey recalls another incident. The doors in question are four in number, and are the three leading into the re-vestry, and one into the Chapel of the Pyx, anciently the royal treasury. Here, as in other instances cited, the skin has been worn by the action of time, or peeled by the curiosity of visitors, from the more exposed portions of the surfaces, but under the iron clamps and hinges it has been preserved, and scientific examination has decided definitely in favour of its claim to be human skin.

The Westminster story, which the late Dean Stanley recalls in his "Historic Memorials of Westminster Abbey," and which he deems to be sufficiently supported by facts, is as follows:—" In the year 1303, King Edward I. was in Scotland, prosecuting that war of subjection which was so nearly successful, when news came to him that his store of 'the sinews of war,' which had been placed in the Treasury at Westminster, had been stolen. Six years before, having exhausted his supplies in his almost continuous hostilities with Wales, Scotland, and France, the King had to raise fresh sums for the prosecution of his plans of conquest. Both clergy and laity had seized the opportunity to press for redress of grievances, and the King had confirmed Magna Charta and the

Charter of Forests, and had in other ways complied with their demands. It is reasonable, therefore, to suppose that in return the people had contributed liberally to the needs of the Kingdom, and that a large amount of money in consequence lay at Westminster.

"On the discovery of the robbery, forty-eight monks of the Abbey, together with the Lord Abbot himself, were arrested and thrown into the Tower, where they were kept while a thorough investigation of the circumstances took place. The result was the acquittal and release of most of the accused; it was, however, proved that one, Richard de Podicate, had made off with the money, being aided and abetted by persons of no less position in the Abbey than the sub-prior and the sacristan. Upon these men condign punishment was inflicted, after such sort, it would appear, that fragments of their skin to this day remain at Westminster as a warning to the robbers of Church and State."

In all these cases we find a record of a barbarous and hideous punishment inflicted for an aggravated act of robbery. In the earlier instances cited, the crime was sacrilege, the furniture of the Church itself being carried off; in this last one, the resources of the State were plundered after they had been placed in a measure under the protection of the Church, and the thieves were those whose duty it was to guard them. It would probably be useless to seek for statutes which ordered, or customs which sanctioned, such a frightful doom as that of flaying alive, even in those rough days, and in the cases of such crimes. In the earlier instances, it is more probable that it was the summary act of a mob stung to frenzy by repeated wrongs, and in the last, the judgment of a stern and justly indignant monarch, to whom a life spent in bloodshed had left but little pity for the agony of those who baulked his will, or marred his schemes.

Animals of the Church, in Wood, Stone, and Bronze.

By T. Tindall Wildridge.

THE presence of the animal representations so frequent in ecclesiastical architecture, and in some degree the forms of those representations, are mainly due to the deterioration at a remotely ancient period of the purer worship of a great deity—the sun. Of this god, adored by early man, various material forms were used as symbols, to which in many instances the worship contracted. The poets by their personification of attributes and emblematic figures were the first to impose the yoke of literalism upon mankind, which the priests, by their different use of exactly the same means in a more advanced mental atmosphere, did much to remove. The early churchmen, following the pagan leaders of thought, saw in every creature, its functions and its characteristics, the symbol of a spiritual or moral meaning applicable to man and his destiny.

Some symbols are great and enduring types, others insignificant and more or less absurd.

Students of ecclesiastical zoology owe a debt of gratitude to Mr. E. P. Evans for his book* on the subject, which can henceforth scarcely be touched without reference to the work. It is not easy to explain the unreal, or to classify what seem at first sight the fanciful conceptions of a non-system in which every worker, were he tyro or master, was justified in evolving fresh conceptions and combinations, though none appears to have fully availed himself of the liberty. Classic art and lore are two of the chief channels by which symbolic representations reached Western Europe, and the want of precision or determination in the present subject is much akin to the vagueness and contradiction abounding in classic mythology itself. Thus the Greeks had three hundred epithets, mostly attributive, and wonderfully diverse, for Jupiter; with the Greeks the left hand was unlucky, but with the Romans both lucky and unlucky. So in mediæval symbolism the proneness to use the same figure for quite opposite purposes, according to the fancied exigencies of the moment, has left us a multitude of casual half-meanings from which to sift a reasonable scheme.

* Animal Symbolism in Ecclesiastical Architecture, by E. P. Evans. William Heineman, London, 1896.

The cause, doubtless, of such a curious state of things being possible in classic times was the final popular semi-absence of real belief in the care or interest the gods had in man, or belief even in the existence of the myriad gods themselves. As the channel was muddy, the waters proved not clear.

We cannot accept Grimm's decision that the whole mystery of the use of animal symbolism had its root in an ancient animal-worship founded on fear. In support of the attribution of supernatural, and therefore sacred, character to the brutes, it is alleged that they were not called by their real names, but propitiated by various flattering epithets, as "gold foot," "broad brow," "flash eye," "forest brother," and the like. Yet there may not be in the use of such terms anything but the hereditary outcome of the poetic temperament which characterises the Aryan race, the tendency of which was to speak of things by an attribute rather than a name, by allusion than by statement. Thus, long before the founding of Athens, the Aryan poet described the dawn clouds as red cows, and noonday clouds as flocks of sheep. So, too, in later classic days, when it was sought to convey the idea of a man being hanged, he was shewn seated in a swing; the word prison was rarely used, house being employed instead; Acteon was not shewn metamorphosed into a stag torn by dogs, but simply seated on a deer-skin! This poetic hinting survives to our day, and in mediæval representation is best exampled by the manner in which the martyrs are delineated, each, for the most part, hale and hearty, but bearing the instrument or means by which he met his death. Gothic crudeness stepped in when St. Thomas, to all appearance with the usual epidermis, is shewn carrying his flayed-off skin in a basket. Other considerations are not wanting which weigh against the assertion of ancient man's universal fear of the beasts. The earliest art work of man yet discovered is a rude sketch scratched upon a bone; it is a picture of the chase, in which Man is the hunter. In every phase of savagery extant, Man is the hunter, not the hunted. Even under such extreme conditions as go to prove fear, as in the case of the Indian tiger, the fear is not veneration; it is a fear qualified by intense hatred and the employment of traps, pitfalls, and other anti-worship engines. Where supernatural character is credited, as in the case of the hyena, there is a fear of killing him, but he is not worshipped. Moreover, in innumerable instances of animal-worship, the gods include animals, birds, and insects, as well as trees, plants, minerals, etc., that have in nature neither marked noxious or beneficial influence. In all real animal worship there may be a large element of the idea of incarnation, but this would probably be late, and added to the primæval teachings of symbolism. Had fear been essential to animal worship, those beasts only which are night prowlers and powerful would, we might expect, be found as the objects of worship.

The line of the symbolists seems to be unbroken. When the early Gothic builders began their labour, they found ready to their hands a rich collection of ornament come down from the Classic, which had in its turn seized and mannerised the designs of the East. But when the builders of Western Europe woke up to the consciousness of how much could be done in architecture with ornament, and evolved the Decorated style, they took not only all that was to be found in the work of their predecessors but ran through wider fields of literature and folk-lore and of Nature, entering with zeal, and according to their various national idiosyncracies, renewing what they found, in lasting forms of wood, stone, and bronze.

ANIMALS OF THE CHURCH.

In one sense compound forms might be said to be, *par excellence*, "the Animals of the Church," for they are to be met scarcely anywhere else but within the Church's jurisdiction. Though outside the scope of this article, one example may be given. It represents a goat or sheep's head hooded, with the body of a goose and the feet of a beast of prey. It is from a door moulding at Notre Dame, Paris, and is an instance of the difficulties which beset classification of mere fruits of fancy.

Many of the subjects of the mediæval church-carver are derived from symbols of sun-worship. One of the most frequent and recognisable of these is a design found on classic tombs, Asiatic cylinders, ancient tesselated pavements, etc.,—the sun-myth in which the powers of darkness watch the altar of the sun, being simply figurative of each day being environed by nights. The general delineation is that of two eagles, but occasionally they are dragons or griffins, and in the numerous instances where we

GOAT-HEAD, NOTRE DAME, PARIS.

meet the subject in our churches, the altar form is lost or mis-represented. In a capital of Romanesque work at Berne, the devourers of day are two wyverns, *i.e.*, eagles whose tails are those of scorpions or dragons. The altar has shrunk into a fruit at which they peck. In a miserere carving in Ripon Minster we find the fruit form of the same type—of blackberry appearance, with a deep calyx—but developed into a whole tree of clusters. Other carvings are similar. In one in Beverley Minster the dark devourers are shown as two swans, the *ara* here being retained as either a circular altar-form, from which the birds peck at the ashes of the fire, or as a vase of seed, according as we believe the artist to have, or have not, known his subject. Whether the fool's hooded head, at which two birds peck (also at Beverley) may be regarded as Sol is questionable, though it will bear such interpretation.

DARKNESS DEVOURING LIGHT,
ST. MARTIN'S, BERNE.

In the dragon we have a great figure, belonging to the cult of sun-worship. He was the principle

ANIMALS OF THE CHURCH. 175

of darkness, and his chief name in the old sun-myth was Typhon. Whether there is any foundation for his general form to be found among the terrible reptiles of the Pliocene age, which the geology of the future may shew to have slightly overlapped the advent of Man, can scarcely, with safety, be conjectured, yet the similarity of type met in all ages and countries would seem to point to something more than the ordinary transmission

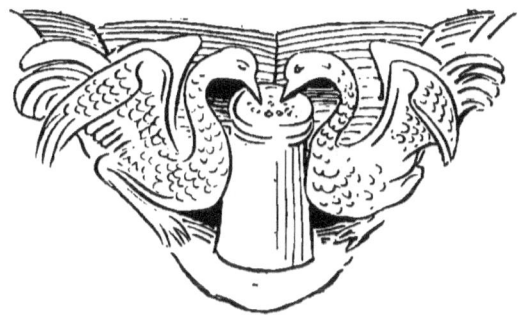

DARKNESS DEVOURING LIGHT, BEVERLEY.

of an invented idea of what never was. The form of the dragon may be said to be that of a long-necked crocodile, winged and with supernal activity and malignity; there are, however, a large number of variants. In the old myth, Typhon is the desert, or winter, the period of darkness; he is slain by Horus (*Hur*, light, from the Sanscrit *ush*, to burn) the sun-god, *i.e.*, the approach of Spring. Horus became a personal god with the Egyptians, who held his festival, consonantly with his attributes, at the beginning of Spring, the precise day being the 23rd of April. The Greeks fed their fancy with the same myth covering the same natural phenomenon; Horus became Apollo who slew the Python; Perseus, the dragon-killer, is another personification of the sun as the winter-slayer. Thence descending to the middle ages, we find the same thing figured by the legendary slaughter of the dragon Fafnir by the hero Sigurd. Here the subject received a kind of sub-division in ancient times. Floods were the most disastrous effects of winter, and in the greater care of land in the middle ages, these were especially noticed and fought against. Mediæval records teem with accounts of floods, embanking, and the like. Now the great danger of a river flood is found constantly alluded to as a dragon, and various persons, who more or less effectually embanked, or otherwise prevented the recurrence of floods, are stated to have slain dragons. Even in the classic figurative history, the Python is said to have been the name of a river, and the evil thing slain by Perseus was a water-dragon. Of the mediæval dragons slain by the saints (who took the place of the classic

ANIMALS OF THE CHURCH.   177

heroes in fable and story) two have names. One of these was the Dragon Gargouille, which ravaged the country round the Seine, and was said to have been slain by St. Romain of Rouen. Gargouille simply means a waterspout or gutter, and is the same word as the Gargoyle of our churches. The other was the Dragon Tarasque, which St. Martha killed at Aix-la-Chapelle. Tarasque is a word derived from the verb *tarir*, to drain, to dry up. There was another dragon which had its haunt in the Loire, and was slain by St. Florent. St. Philip slew a dragon at Hierapolis; three saints, St. Cado, Maudet, and Paull, slew Breton dragons; St. Keyne slew the Cornish dragon, while Donatus, Sts. Clement of Metz, George, Margaret, Michael, and Samson, Archbishop of Dol, and Pope Sylvester, all similarly distinguished themselves. Some of these are merely local, but among them is, doubtless, more than one instance of the cropping up of the old sun-myth. The survivor is certainly St. George, who definitely representing Horus and Apollo, is a notable instance of Christian adoption of a Pagan myth in its concrete form. The dragon borne in the Rogation processions is Typhon himself. Whether the word George (*i.e.*, Earth-worker) was selected as an allowable attribute of the sun may be open to objection, but St. George's day is the 23rd of April, as in the case of Horus, who also was shewn mounted in Egyptian presentments. The carving here drawn is, however, of a St. George who has dismounted, and is given as affording a good example of what is sometimes seen in the paintings of the middle ages and elsewhere — the insignificant size of the vanquished reptile. This carving is on one of the interesting bench ends in the choir of Holy Trinity Church, Hull.

ST. GEORGE AND DRAGON, HOLY TRINITY CHURCH, HULL.

Where St. George slew the Dragon, is not known, for it has been shewn that the Dragon's Hill, in Berkshire, is an incorrect assignment, the "dragon" there killed, being the Celtic Pendragon Naud, defeated and slain by Cedric the Saxon.

In its later symbolism as shewing the evil one

ANIMALS OF THE CHURCH.

as a person, the dragon form is largely utilized with considerable modifications, to render the figure more or less human, a very suggestive necessity; the example is one of the numerous similar figures which adorn the Cathedral of Notre Dame, Paris.

Not often is the dragon shewn without wings; a seat-carving at Beverley shews him thus, while on his back is seated a hare, the appropriate symbol of (among other things, including libidinousness) timidity. The hare has evidently the whip-hand of the evil one, and it is only necessary to find a name for the halter or reins with which he is being guided, to offer a forcible lesson.

SATAN, NOTRE DAME, PARIS.

Dragons are perhaps the most prolific of all the designs, for there can be no doubt at any time of the signification of the figures; a lion may mean the good or the bad, but a dragon is ever evil. Devouring men, in combat with lions, with monsters, with men, and with one another, or merely mocking Creation with their ugliness, dragons are ubiquitous. The word dragon is derived through the Latin *draco*, and the Greek *drakōn*, from the

Sanscrit *dric*, to see, from the power the reptile was said to have of destroying, like the basilisk, by the glare of its terrible eyes.

The Serra is a sea-dragon, which, excepting in the head, has all other characteristics of those of a goose or swan. An example at Beverley has in its breast the face of a man. The original Serra is a winged saw-fish.

The dragon was a Keltic ensign. Henry VII.

HARE AND DRAGON, BEVERLEY.

in honour of his Welsh descent made it one of the supporters of the royal arms; it retained its place until the accession of James I., who supplanted it with the unicorn.

The lion may be said in the abstract to be symbolic of sovereignty or power, and its use or accompanying decoration determine whether it is intended as a type of good or evil.

The lion affords, in one of its frequent church

symbols met on the continent, a curious instance of erroneous natural history. It was believed that the lioness brought forth her young dead, and that after three days the lion by howling over them woke them to life, and this led representations of the incident to be taken as a suitable symbol of Christ and the Resurrection. Perhaps the belief arose, from a hasty observation of the fact that the male lion sometimes kills his new-born young. Usually the female drives him away for a short time to obviate the catastrophe. The lion was also fabled never to close its eyes, a belief engendered by its nocturnal habits. This peculiarity led to

KNOCKER AT ADEL CHURCH.

its being placed at the doors of the sanctuaries, either as figures at the sides of the approach, or as heads in the knocker or hagoday. The persistency of design of these bronze knockers is somewhat curious. In many, the lion's head is shewn with a human head at the opening at the mouth. This may simply be devised to keep the ring-knocker in its place, or it may be a sort of hell's mouth, and have a symbolical meaning, warning the fugitive taking refuge in the sanctuary, or perhaps his pursuers, of the penalties of trespass. But too much stress must not be laid upon this, as it is so evident that they are either from one another, or have a common original. Thus we see at Adel church, Yorkshire, All Saints', York, and St. Gregory's, Norwich, three bronze knockers, all of the fourteenth century, in which every detail is of the same design. The lion mask, without the human head in the mouth, is seen in the earlier hagoday at the south door of Durham Cathedral, dating from 1140.

KNOCKER AT ALL SAINTS' CHURCH, YORK.

All the above examples have sharp-pointed ears; it is interesting to compare the fine lion knocker of Mayence, which has round ears, and though in other respects similar to the Durham hagoday, is evidently of much later date.

The lion at the feet of the recumbent effigies on tombs, signified at one time that the soul had its foot on Satan, but later, was the indication of robust hope, confidence, and vigilance: hence a dog occasionally holds the place. A lion at Hazeley, Oxfordshire, caresses the foot of the mailed effigy.

The representations of hell's mouth by the open jaws of a beast, most frequently use the dragon, but sometimes the lion is met. The lion is generally to be taken as the emblem of the resurrection, and is assigned as the emblem of St. Mark, because his chief object was to give an account of the resurrection of Christ.

KNOCKER, ST. GREGORY'S CHURCH, NORWICH.

The cat has no high significance, and is generally found in domestic or folk-lore subjects of a comic nature. Two examples are given from Beverley. In one a monkey, having doubtless observed some process of combing or currying, occupies itself with combing a cat. In the other we have evidence of the long continuance of our nursery rhyme :—

> "Hey diddle, diddle,
> The cat and the fiddle,"

which probably supplies a meaning to the "diddle" portion of the distich. A cat is charming four mice with the dulcet strains of the viol, while apparently she keeps a watchful and appreciative eye upon the largest and fattest. A companion carving shews her seizing her prey. In a miserere at Wells Cathedral, a carving of earlier date also shews us the mediæval cat and fiddle. Probably the verse is the relic of a metrical satire on the worship of the moon. Another Wells carving shews us a hawk preying upon a hare.

KNOCKER, DURHAM CATHEDRAL.

The dog is seen at Beverley helping himself to a fish from a cooking pot, while a man turns from a blazing fire to chastise him; in another carving a dog is gnawing a bone. The dogs we find in carvings of the middle ages, appear to be a breed more robust than the ren or greyhound, but of that species.

The character of the monkey was well grasped by mediæval artists, in whose time, indeed, the animal was more common as a household pet than at present. The same series of carvings at Beverley as that from which the cat is taken, includes a monkey riding a horse, pursued by the enraged owner, another holding a child in swaddling clothes, another examining a bottle after the manner of the doctor

LION KNOCKER, MAYENCE.

prognosticators, another chasing a cat with a club; while a good carving illustrates the story of the pedlar who was attacked by apes, who held him down while they distributed his hamper of wares. Others shew him being trained under the whip, playing the bagpipes while a bear dances, and using a cat as bagpipes by biting its tail. There is also an example of what appears to be the cynocephali (*simia innus*) or dog-headed monkey, regarded by the Egyptians as a sacred animal. A seat-carving at Bristol shews a monkey on horseback, running off with stolen bags of grain.

The pedlar scene and the ape doctor is also shewn at Manchester and Bristol, where likewise are stone sculptures of the ape and fox episodes.

The pig is frequently met in church ornament,

MONKEY AND CAT, BEVERLEY.

as probably being an animal very familiar to the sight of the artists, as well as possessing considerable symbolic import. It is most often used in burlesque representations. At Durham, Ripon, and Beverley choirs, are dances of pigs, in which the sow plays the bagpipes while her little ones trip their light fantastic hoofs. The Beverley carving is supported by two other pig-sculptures, in one a sow is shewn saddled, in the other playing a harp. There is a significance in this, for a pregnant sow was sacrificed yearly at the winter solstice, in, it is said, honour of Mercury, the inventor of the harp. The Druids also sacrificed a sow at the winter solstice, doubtless a relic of sun-worship. A pig was sacrificed by the Athenians at the commencement of the deliberature and judicial assemblies held bi-monthly, and with them a sow, being, it is said, a corn-destroyer, was sacrificed yearly to Ceres. The hog is the symbol of St. Anthony, stated to have been in his youth a swineherd, and the smallest pig of a litter is sometimes called an "Anthony pig." The example engraved is from one of the croches or elbow rests in the Choir of Beverley Minster.

THE CAT AND THE FIDDLE, BEVERLEY.

The beaver when met in church work is generally found in a curled up and apparently sleeping attitude. But the meaning of the position is that the animal is biting off the castoreum bags, which it was fabled to do when hunted, so that its pursuers might take them, the object of their chase, and so relinquish further pursuit. The town arms of Beverley shew the beaver in the posture for this self-excision. It is also met there as a cognizance in the Minstrel's Chain, and on a seal, as having wings, displayed, and a carving of it on a bench end in the minster shews the same disposition. The beaver is a symbol of Christ in the point of view of self-sacrifice.

The earliest carving of an elephant in England is said to be at Exeter. A miserere at Beverley Minster, in which the animal bears a howdah, and one or more bold carvings on the heads of bench-ends in the same church are among the very few examples of church representations of elephants. The elephant is one of the attributive names of Buddha, and is an emblem of Christ. Mediæval natural history relates that the female elephant brought forth her young in the water, in which respect it is a symbol of baptism. It is also sometimes an emblem of chastity.

THE CAT AND FIDDLE, WELLS.

Deer are generally shewn in simple natural attitudes and situations. A hart or hind signified solitude, and is the emblem of St. Hubert, like-

ANIMALS OF THE CHURCH.

wise of St. Julian and St. Eustace. Hunting scenes are not uncommon.

The camel is the symbol of submission; it appears on seat carvings at Boston and Beverley.

The serpent symbolizes, as well as the evil principle, also regeneration, and the love of Christ. In Egyptian and classic arts, the serpent signified reviving health, as in the beautiful

HAWK AND HARE, WELLS.

symbolic figures of the well-known Portland or Barberini Vase of late classic date.

The otter and the ichneumon, as slayers of the crocodile, are figures of the power of Christ exercised against Satan.

The panther is a symbol of Christ, so also is the plover.

The wolf signified lewdness; the hyena unnatural vice.

The squirrel is a figure of the striving with man of the Holy Spirit.

The unicorn, "whose horn is worth a city" says the Gule's Horn Book of 1609, on account of its being an infallible detectant and counteracter of poison, and a certain cure for epilepsy, was considered to live only in remote solitudes. The only hope of slaying or securing him was to use as bait a pure maiden, in whose lap he would

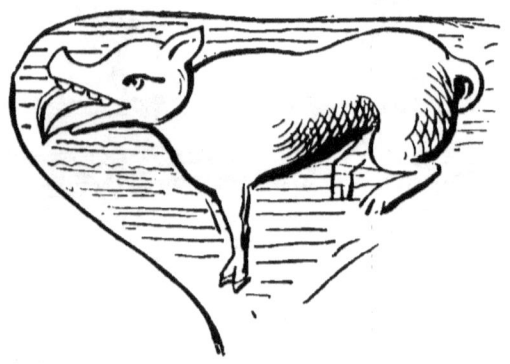

PIG BEVERLEY MINSTER.

nestle his head, and sleep to his destruction. Thus it became the symbol of chastity and purity, and was the emblem of the Virgin Mary, of St. Agatha, and St. Justinia. The horns, anciently prized as those of the unicorn, where it has been possible to submit them to modern examination, prove to be those of the narwhal. Like the lion the unicorn signified both the good and bad, according to the inversion of meaning. The unicorn is not very frequent as a church animal. The example drawn, which is one of three at Beverley, is given because of its graceful horse-like form.

The sheep is often shewn in pastoral scenes, as shearings, etc. The cow and horse also generally figure in simple episodes of everyday life.

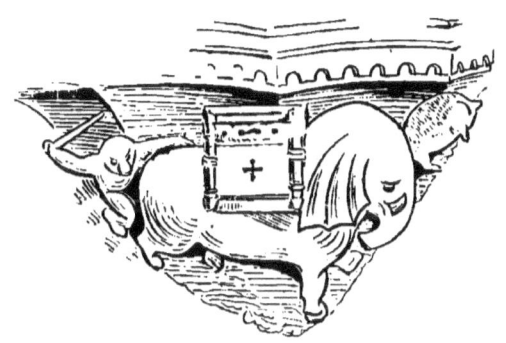

WIT AND WRIGHT, MONKEY, ELEPHANT AND PIG, BEVERLEY MINSTER.

Two rams in the Beverley choir butt at each other so that their horns each form half of the astronomical sign ♈ (Aries, the Ram).

The bear is generally treated as an animal familiar to the sight of the artists in situations of training, conveyance, trick performing, baiting, and is shewn muzzled. In a few cases the bear is used symbolically as a type of Satan.

The whale, in some departments of oriental

lore, is fabled to bear up the world, and that there is a constant chance of its diving, to which it is persuaded by the evil one, and so overwhelming the globe. This whale takes the place of the turtle or tortoise in Indian and the serpent in Scandinavian mythology, and points to the deluge theory, and perhaps tends to shew an early and forgotten appreciation of the gradual change of poles, and the necessary consequences, so admirably embodied in one of Huxley's most suggestive Lay Sermons.

UNICORN, BEVERLEY MINSTER.

No account of the church animals would be complete without mention of the fox — Reynard the crafty — whom all affect to condemn, but who is respected for his successes, and is the most popular and most sung of all the animals.

In the fox-carving here drawn, the fox is shewn, without robes, in a pulpit, preaching to a goose and a cock; his forepaws and what they may have held are broken off; but the cunning conveyed into his countenance preaches the whole

ANIMALS OF THE CHURCH.

lesson. There are many similar examples; at Beverley Reynard is in full canonicals; among the misereres of the lesser church of Beverley (St. Mary's), at Boston, Bristol, Nantwich, Ripon and Sherborne, are carvings of the fox preaching or hanging. Here also he is carved as prowling near two sleeping geese; as being hanged on a square gallows by a number of birds; as being resuscitated by an ape, who unties the rope from

THE PREACHING FOX, RIPON.

his neck, the rope terminating, to shew his awakening, in a Wake knot.

It would be interesting to find the original of the design in which the fox is shewn preaching to a congregation of geese, while he is addressing them, as appears by a label, in these words: "Testis est mihi Deus, quam cupiam vos omnes visceribus meis," from the first chapter of Philippians. In all the preaching scenes, this somewhat improper punning address may be supposed to be uttered. It is noted as met in carving, in stained glass, and in manuscripts.

Perhaps the oldest animal carving in this country is at Aldborough Church, Yorkshire (St. Bartholomew, probably originally Holy Trinity), built by Ulf, a Danish or Saxon lord of Holderness, who died in the reign of Edward the Confessor. It represents, in somewhat graceful lines, three animals, which appear to be a pair and their little one. Their species is so doubtful that they may be either vulpine or bovine.

SAXON ANIMALS, ALDBOROUGH.

Snails are occasionally met in church decoration. A snail at Boston is being driven up a hill by a monk; another at Beverley is being stabbed by a fashionably-attired gentleman of the fifteenth century. These are of different import from the mention of the snail in the romance of Reynard, where he is the standard-bearer, because he could so well scale walls! The Papal Church claimed to drive away snails by means of excommunicatory cursing.

The eagle, like the lion, affords a multitude of symbolisms. Its marked change of plumage after moulting gave rise to the fable of its renewing its youth by plunging into a pool, used as the symbol of baptism, and by cremation. This latter idea, evolving the phœnix, gives another chief emblem of sun-worship. The Jews regarded it as an emblem of the renewal of life, as did the Romans, who carved it upon their burial-urns. There are curious coincidences in the language-changes of the words which are instances of the vagueness of symbolic cults. The Hebrew word *chul* means both sand and phœnix, and the Greek for both phœnix and palmtree is the same. The confusion is seen in Job xxix. 18, and Psalm xcii. 12, and in numerous carvings where the phœnix is shewn seated on a palmtree. Both are used in Christian art as symbolic of regeneration.

The pelican, "whose sons are nurs't with bloode," was a favourite subject of the wood-carver. The bird's alleged habit of drawing blood from its own breast to feed its young, caused it to be taken as the special emblem of Christ, and the symbol generally of Christian piety. Considerable trouble has been taken to shew that the pelican is an error for flamingo, because the latter bird can produce from the crop a blood secretion in an act of feeding, and because many ancient sculptures shew the bird as much resembling a flamingo as a pelican. The pelican cannot be thus surrendered. There is no bird from a dodo to a crow which the inaccuracy of the church artist has not, in one instance or another, made his pelican resemble more than the actual pelican form. The true explanation is that the pelican's beak is tipped with red or a reddish colour, its breast is frequently bare of feathers, and it has a habit of reposing its beak on its neck and breast, giving a considerable impression of self-wounding. In suggesting a re-reading as "flamingo" it was not taken into account that the pelican was said to feed its young with blood from its *breast*, and that the idea is one of sacrifice. Thus in " Birds Forbidden :" " She stabbeth deep her breast, self murtheresse through fondnesse to her broode," as parents do everyday. Moreover, it is not necessary to find exact prototypes for all the attributes of the church animals, though frequently they have a foundation in imperfect observation of natural features. The seat of the Archbishop of York, in Beverley Minster, has a beautiful example of this symbol, and there is another on the canopy. The seat of the Precentor of the Minster has also, among other things, the same subject, with the young pelicans in a basket. It is also the subject of a miserere at Boston.

The cock was the emblem of St. Peter; and of vigilance, of the Resurrection, courage, and liberality. Among the Beverley misereres are two cocks sparring on a barrel, a literal rendering of the old expression, cock-a-hoop. In another a cock is carved above the words *clericus fabrici;* this was John Sparke, who, in 1520, would, no doubt, have the supervision of the execution of these misereres. The vigilant bird is a well-chosen emblem to associate with a clerk of works. The cock, like the dragon, was a Welsh badge. Mr. Evans has misunderstood the above name, reading Sparke as "Wake," and points an inference in connection with the bird and the name. John Sparke was the Receiver-General and Warden of the Fabric of Beverley Minster. The examination of some others of the Beverley carvings by Mr. Evans appears to have been hasty, as his description in those cases are not marked by his usual accuracy. The cock was a Welsh and Gothic badge. The cock was dedicated to Apollo, Mars, and Mercury, and was sacrificed to Esculapius; all these, however, are one and the same, the solar deity, and the connection is the salutation given by the cock to the rising sun.

The owl is the symbol of wisdom, emblem of Minerva, and the tutelary bird of Athens, but mediævally the symbol of darkness and unbelief, and, like the raven, a symbol of the Jews. At Beverley it is seen attacked by a possè of smaller birds, as not infrequently occurs in nature.

The hawk is most frequently seen in what may be termed natural scenes. At Wells a hawk is preying upon a hare; at Beverley it is hunting a bat. It is curious to note that the hawk in mediæval carving has generally a round and parrot-like head, the true falcon shape being rarely achieved.

Both the crow and the turtle-dove signify constancy and devotion, having alike the reputation of never taking a second mate.

The heron is a type of wisdom, the thrush of the grace of God.

The partridge, from a supposed or real inclination to rear the young of others, is a type of benevolence.

The hen and chickens is the emblem of God's providence, and one of the special emblems of Christ; it was frequently adopted as a device in mediæval times.

The raven was the symbol of concord and long life; but also in the later, and more involved, symbolism of the Fathers, typifies the Jews.

The dove was the type of conjugal fidelity; of rest, peace, and salvation; and every portion of its frame had its special lesson.

Birds in general were considered symbolic of the souls of martyrs; souls in general are shewn by the nakedness of the figures.

The fish is frequently met in the church. It was the symbol of chastity and one of the emblems of the Virgin Mary, as well as of Christ; the Greek word being used as the sacred acrostic, thus:

I èsus	Jesus
C hristus	Christ
TH eou	of God
U ios	the Son
S oter	Saviour.

The elliptical or ovoidal form of the fish is used as an emblem known as the Vesica Piscis (fish-bladder); windows were made of this form, and it has been held that it is not without muliebraic reference.

The fish in classic mythology was credited with acting as the ferryman to bear the souls of the dead to the islands of bliss. It was a symbol of

Venus (and hence of the Virgin Mary, who took in Christian imagery the place of Aphrodite), and the use of Friday as a fish-eating day gave it the name it bears, *dies veneris* (French, *vendredi*), akin to the Saxon Fria-day, Fria being the Germanic equivalent of Venus. An eagle seizing a fish from the water is to be seen on the Norman doorway of Ribbeford Church, Worcestershire; the same is met among Keltic symbols, the attributed meaning being taking of the elect by Christ.

Other animals are met in church carving, but the chief have been mentioned, and sufficient to illustrate man's aptitude for seizing on material forms to enforce on his fellows some spiritual or moral sentiment, or some fact scarcely patent to the general intelligence. We have, especially, seen that where long descent could be traced, mediæval symbolism rises out from the ashes of ancient myths, which can sometimes be seen to be relics of great primæval conceptions.

Queries in Stones.

By the Rev. Francis Haslewood, f.s.a.

MANY of our Parish Churches bear, in their architectural details, traces of customs and usages which, though general in early times, have, in the course of centuries, not only become obsolete, but their exact character is now wholly unknown. For example, low side-windows are still a subject for controversy among well-known antiquaries, and several niches and squints still remain, the exact use of which have baffled some of our most learned authorities upon sacred archæology. To these may be added the gargoyles which abound on the exterior, and the curiously carved grotesque figures which often disfigure the interior of many of our village churches. A remarkable example of this is to be found in what is now a remote village, though possessing a charter for a weekly market, granted by Queen Elizabeth. The church is that of Smarden, situate in the Weald of Kent, about nine miles from Ashford. Here, in this remarkable church (dedicated to S. Michael), popularly known as the "Barn of Kent" (from the singular construction of its wide roof without side aisles or tie beams), is found a Grotesque Head, in the north wall of the nave, near the eastern end, at about eight feet from the ground. It is supported by two corbels of early character, and the figure, though without shoulders, has hands distending the mouth. On the arms are bracelets. The material of which it is carved is Bethersden marble, a stone found in the locality, which takes an excellent polish, and on this account the fonts in several neighbouring parishes are formed of it. The use of this curious head, which cannot be described as comical, is open to conjecture, as to whether it was in some way connected with the mediæval superstitions in regard to exorcism, gargoyles on the exterior of churches being known to have such reference. There are no other figures of a similar nature in any part of the church; and in this particular spot it certainly could not have been introduced by way of ornament, as the monster is hideous in the extreme. Another suggestion has been offered, namely, that it had some connection with the Easter and Whitsun ales. Those who favour this theory quote as an example the figure on the porch of Chalk Church, Kent, which is supposed to illustrate the humours of a church ale. Then again, these church ales afford matter for speculation, but very little seems to be really known about them. Popular belief goes to

GROTESQUE FIGURE, SMARDEN CHURCH.

show that in pre-reformation times the church then, as in our own day, was constantly requiring funds, and these were partly raised by the sale of ale, then the common English beverage, just as money is obtained in this nineteenth century by selling tea at the refreshment stalls, so general at the bazaars held for charitable purposes. An engraving of the grotesque head is given in the "Memorials of Smarden," which we reproduce.

Our thanks are due to the writer of the foregoing notes for the loan of the illustration used in this chapter.

EDITOR.

Pictures in Churches.

BY THE REV. GEO. S. TYACK, B.A.

TO the thoughtful man of to-day it must be almost inconceivable that so much controversy should ever have raged about the use of pictures in churches. At the present time there is scarcely even a nonconformist community that has not practically admitted the propriety of their use, although in some quarters an illogical, indeed an incomprehensible, distinction seems to have been drawn between transparent pictures in the windows, and paintings on the walls. The Puritans of past centuries were most narrow-minded in their condemnation of art, but they were also more consistent. To them apparently all art was a sacrament of the devil, whereby he entangled and ruined the souls of men. Milton, it is true, felt the hallowing influences of art, and in his *Il Penseroso* sings the praise of architecture, painting, and music—

> "Let my due feet never fail
> To walk the studious Cloisters' pale,
> And love the high embowered roof
> With antique pillars mossy proof,

> And storied windows richly dight
> Casting a dim religious light;
> There let the pealing organ blow
> To the full-voiced quire below,
> In service high and anthem clear,
> As may with sweetness through mine ear
> Dissolve me into ecstacies,
> And bring all heaven before mine eyes."

But these were the thoughts of the young Milton of twenty-five or six, the author of the Mask of *Comus*, and the entertainment *Arcades*; not of that man of sterner mould whom we meet in his later works.

It was natural that in the first centuries the Christians should exhibit great caution in the use of pictures. The Jews who had embraced the new faith clung for the most part tenaciously to the details of the older law, and to those traditions which their "eldars" had founded upon it, as is abundantly proved by many passages in the Acts of the Apostles and the Pauline Epistles. On the other hand the church would certainly realize that great care was needed in the treatment of converts from Paganism, accustomed to the worship of all manner of sculptured or painted idols, lest even pictures symbolical of the Christian faith should be abused rather than used. That the primitive church was not, however, afraid to employ art as a handmaid, is proved by the Roman catacombs. The Catacomb of St. Priscilla, dates from Apostolic times, or at latest only just subsequently to them, the Catacomb of St. Callixtus is probably the next in age, and is not very much later; and in these, as well as in other sections of these sacred Christian cemeteries, pictures meet us on all hands. Simple studies of Our Lord as the Good Shepherd, examples of the emblematic vine, and other subjects not beyond the talents of a poor and largely illiterate community, are some of the first specimens of Christian art. Representations of Old Testament scenes, more or less emblematic in treatment, and later of New Testament persons and events, followed.

There is evidence, it must be admitted, of a local suspicion of the use of pictures even in early times, for which there may have been special and local reasons. A council held at Elvira, in Spain, in the year 305, passed a canon declaring that "pictures ought not to be in churches, lest that which is worshipped and adored be painted upon the walls." Yet in less than a century we have the description written by

St. Paulinus (who curiously enough had spent much time in Spain) of the elaborate pictures in his church at Nola in Italy. Scenes from Old Testament history adorned the walls, and in the apse was an emblematic design of the Holy Trinity, and another of the Cross. "In all its mystery," says the saintly bishop, "shines forth the Trinity; Christ stands in the lamb, the Father's voice thunders from Heaven, and as a dove flies forth the Holy Ghost." The Cross was encircled with a crown of light, and the Apostles typified by a flock of doves. These pictures were in mosaic, as were many, if not most, of the early icons in the west, while those in the east are more commonly the work of the painter.

Amongst early writers of authority who refer to pictures in churches, we find St. Augustine of Hippo, who speaks of figures of St. Peter and St. Paul, of the martyrdom of St. Stephen, and the sacrifice of Abraham. Asterius, Bishop of Amasea, tells us that close to the spot where the relics of St. Euphemia, the martyr, were preserved, "the painter by means of his art, and to the best of his abilities, exactly portrayed on his canvas the martyr's whole history, and hung it in such a position as to be seen by all." The purpose of these pictures is plainly set forth by a disciple of St John Chrysostom, St. Nilus the Abbot, namely, "that they who cannot read the Holy Scriptures, may be able as they look upon the picture to call to mind the noble acts of those who have served God with sincerity," and for this reason the same saint advised the prefect Olympiodorus "to fill the holy temple on all sides with Scripture pictures by the hand of the most skilful artist."

According to some authorities pictures were hung in very early times in the portico of the church, especially for the contemplation of penitents, who were not suffered to advance further into the sacred precincts. An example, which reminds one of this practice, exists at Lutterworth, where three figures are depicted in fresco above the northern door. The local tradition describes them as Queen Phillippa, King Edward III., and John of Gaunt, and avers that the Queen, countenanced by John, is requesting the King to confer the rectory of Lutterworth on John Wyclif. Another account describes the two male figures as those of Edward II. and Edward III. The style of the work is that of the later fourteenth century, and the subject must be admitted to be very doubtful. A not uncommon design for the decoration of the wall over the north door was a figure of St. Christopher bearing the child Christ.

Encouraged by the church a great school of artists sprung up in Mediæval Europe, to whom we owe an incalculable debt of gratitude. The glorious works of the monastic painters, Fra Angelico, Fra Fillipo, and Fra Bartolomeo, of Michael Angelo and Leonardo da Vinci, of Duccio, Botticelli, Correggio, of Raphael, Giorgione, and a hundred more, were most of them produced for the decoration of churches or other ecclesiastical buildings. As illustrations it must suffice to quote the world-famed frescoes of Michael Angelo in the Sistine chapel at Rome, the glowing witnesses to the faith of Fra Angelico at Florence, and the *Last Supper* of Leonardo da Vinci in a convent at Milan, made familiar by means of countless copies. Many examples originally painted for the decoration of churches have found their way in modern times into museums and picture galleries in England or abroad, but every traveller in Europe, and especially in Italy and Spain, is aware of the vast amount of splendid art still to be seen in the cathedrals and monastic churches there.

Undoubtedly our own country, although producing no mediæval painter of mark, availed herself to the full of such opportunities as were afforded her, for the pictorial decoration of her churches. Very few old pictures remain to us, and not many traces or fragments even still exist, but there are enough to show that our forefathers appreciated and used this commonsense method of instruction, until the torrent of Genevan influence in the sixteenth century devastated the sacred art of the country.

The almost incredible suspicion with which all art was regarded by the continental reformers is illustrated by the correspondence of Christopher Hales with some of them. He had given orders for the portraits of six German Protestants to be painted and sent to him, but complains that one Master Gualter had "retained four of them. . . . because there is some danger lest a door shall hereafter be opened to idolatry." He remonstrates in consequence with Gualter, and expresses himself as "greatly surprised" (as indeed he well might be) "that Burcher should persist in thinking that portraits can no wise be painted

with a safe conscience, and a due regard to godliness." When such men as these, fanatical in ignorant scrupulosity, were allowed to advise the bishops and doctors of the English church, there is small wonder that an iconoclastic outbreak was the result. Hooper, in his "Declaration of Christ and His Office" (first published in 1547) admits indeed that "the art of graving and painting is the gift of God"; but he goes on to make the illogical distinction by which so great a means of religious instruction is specially excluded from the church, the home of religion. "To have the picture or image of any martyr or other," he says, "so it be not put in the temple of God, nor otherwise abused, it may be suffered." In the same spirit, Nowell, Dean of St. Paul's, in a catechism published in 1570, while allowing that the second commandment in the Decalogue does not "wholly condemn the arts of painting and portraiture," yet deduces from it the teaching "that it is very perilous to set any images or pictures in churches." When ideas like these were rife, it will cause no surprise to find Hooper issuing, in 1551, injunctions to the clergy of the diocese of Gloucester, to the following effect:—
"Item, that when any glass windows within any

of the churches shall from henceforth be repaired,
or new made, that you do not permit to be
painted or purtured (portrayed) therein the image
of any saint; but if they will have anything
painted, that it be either branches, flowers, or
posies (mottoes) taken out of the holy scripture.
And that ye cause to be defaced all such images
as yet do remain painted upon any of the walls of
your churches, and that from henceforth there be
no more such."

Then doubtless began the glorious era of
whitewash, during which such figures and pictures
as could not be taken away and destroyed were
daubed over with lime. Thus in the accounts of
St. Giles's, Reading, for the year 1560, we find
an entry, "For white liming the roode, 1d."

Here and there, nevertheless, an ancient
painting yet remains to us; some few have been
recovered by the removal of the layers of whitewash under which they had been long concealed;
and something has been done in recent years to
supply the places of some that have been lost.

In the crypt of Canterbury Cathedral is a
quaint painting representing the Nativity of St.
John the Baptist. St. Elizabeth lies on a couch
with the infant Forerunner in her arms, while the

father, St. Zacharias, seated at a table, writes on a scroll his statement that the child's name is John, to the evident astonishment of the assembled neighbours.

At Catfield, Norfolk, some very interesting frescoes have been preserved, by which the space above the arcade on both sides is adorned. The seven sacraments, the seven deadly sins and their appropriate punishments, and various other subjects are here depicted.

In the Galilee Chapel of Durham Cathedral are two figures, perhaps St. Cuthbert and St. Oswald, which have not been certainly identified. In cleaning the walls of the parish church of Crowle, Lincolnshire, at its restoration some ten years since, a mural painting was discovered; but unfortunately, before steps could be taken for its preservation, it crumbled away.

One subject, which apparently was formerly popular in England for the adornment of the space above the chancel arch, was the Last Judgment, known as a Doom.

One such exists in the Chapel of the Holy Cross at Stratford-on-Avon, having been discovered in 1804. The happiness of the blessed, and the tortures of the lost are represented with most realistic force, but the effect produced on a modern spectator is scarcely the one aimed at by the artist. A better example is met with at Lutterworth. The Saviour Himself appears at the top seated in glory upon a rainbow, while two angels with trumpets summon the quick and dead to meet Him. Beneath is the earth, represented as a brown expanse, on which a multitude of graves are seen, from which the dead are issuing—some as skeletons only, some as complete bodies. Two larger angels bearing scrolls are depicted, one on either side of the arch.

A Doom discovered at Wenhaston, Suffolk, in 1892, is especially noteworthy, both on account of the strange manner in which its existence was discovered, and for the intrinsic merits of the composition. It is painted upon an oak partition which fills up the arch above the chancel screen, and is said by competent judges to have been executed about the year 1480. At the Reformation the great crucifix, or rood, with the figures of St. Mary and St. John, which formerly stood against it, were taken down, and the painting was whitewashed, so that all trace, and in time all memory, of it disappeared. About 1860 a hole was cut through one side of this boarding to allow of the passage of a stove-pipe, and, in 1892, the whole screen was pulled down as of no architectural or antiquarian interest, taken to pieces, and thrown into the churchyard, with a view to being entirely removed. By a piece of extraordinary good fortune the following night was exceedingly wet, and by the succeeding morning no small amount of whitewash had been swept from the boards by the pelting rain, and portions of the painting stood manifest to the astonished eyes of the workmen. It is needless to add that after this all the oak was carefully cleaned and replaced, the colours being wonderfully bright, and the whole forming one of the most interesting Dooms extant.

In the middle is a blank space, marking the portion originally covered by the rood; and similar reminders of the figures of St. Mary and St. John are on either side. Above the right arm of the cross is seated the Lord upon a rainbow, as in the Lutterworth Doom; while kneeling in supplication to Him on the left side are the Blessed Virgin and St. John Baptist, the latter identified by his "raiment of camel's hair." The rood with its attendant statues naturally divides the lower portion of the picture into four sections, and of this the artist has availed himself in arranging his

WEHASTON FONT.

subject. On the right side of the shaft of the cross is St. Peter, robed as a pope, receiving the souls of a king, a queen, a cardinal, and a bishop. Still further to the right is a castellated double gateway, at which angels are seen admitting the blessed. On the left-hand side of the rood we see St. Michael weighing souls, while the Devil, "the accuser of the brethren," stands by with a scroll containing presumably his accusations against them. At the extreme left a huge head with gaping jaws, the usual mediæval method of suggesting hell-mouth, appears, into which the lost souls are dragged and pushed. At intervals, in the main design, bodies are seen rising from their graves. For clearness it ought perhaps to be added that the terms right and left are used above as in heraldry, for the opposite sides of the painting, not of the spectator. The portion of the oak which has been cut away contained the figure of an angel summoning the world to judgment, part of his arm and his trumpet being still visible. Several scrolls are inserted in the composition, the lettering of which has disappeared, but no doubt their inscriptions were of the usual kind in such pieces; "Come, ye blessed," "Depart, ye cursed," in the Latin of the Vulgate.

Another Doom, painted like this one on a panel, is preserved in the triforium of Gloucester Cathedral.

In the parish church of South Leigh is an elaborate scheme of pictorial decoration dating from the fifteenth century. The Doom occupies its usual place over the chancel arch, but spreads itself also over the nave walls. Over the arch we have the resurrection of the just and the unjust, who are summoned by angels robed respectively in white and in black, together with Hell-mouth and the usual accessories. Heaven is depicted on the north wall of the nave; a castellated gateway, at which stands St. Peter with his keys, gives admission to the celestial city, the towers and spires of which are seen in the distance. On the south wall of the nave we see St. Michael the Archangel engaged in weighing the souls, and the mystical figure of the " woman clothed with the sun," and having the moon under her feet, is also introduced. On the east wall of the chancel another subject is treated, namely the Annunciation: on the south side of the window is a figure of the Blessed Virgin, standing with upturned eyes and holding a lily, while the divine Dove is seen descending upon her. It seems probable that the effigy of St. Gabriel must at one time have stood on the opposite side, or at any rate that such was the intention. On the north wall of the aisle of the church is a painting of St. Clement of Rome, in full episcopal vestments, with an anchor, the emblem of his martyrdom by drowning. The picture of the Annunciation is the latest of these paintings, all of which were coated with whitewash, and some of them overlaid also with other paintings of a later date.

At the restoration of Blyth Church, near Retford, a doom was discovered in the usual position and of the common type; every effort proved unfortunately fruitless towards preserving it when it was exposed to the air, but a photograph was taken of it before its final disappearance.

About fifteen years ago some quaint paintings were discovered on the south wall of the chancel in the little parish church of Easby, near Richmond, Yorkshire; the subjects being the appearance of the angels to the shepherds, the visit of the Magi, the taking down from the Cross, the entombment of our Lord, and the Resurrection.

Above the arches of the organ-screen at Exeter Cathedral is a series of thirteen curious paintings of ancient date, representing some of the most striking scenes in scriptural history, such as the Creation, Paradise, the Deluge, Solomon's Temple, and events in the life of our Lord, concluding with the descent of the Holy Ghost at Pentecost.

It will have been noticed that of all subjects the Doom was obviously the most common in England, and in considering the value of these paintings as instruments of popular instruction, it must be remembered that, in all the instances here quoted, and probably invariably, they stood in close connection with the Rood. The Wenhaston Doom is peculiar in having had the great crucifix actually fastened to it, but in the other cases the Rood undoubtedly stood on a screen beneath it. The whole arrangement would therefore form a singularly complete expression of the redemptive work of Christ.

In recent years steps have been taken in several places to revive the use of pictures in our churches. The mosaic enrichment of St. Paul's Cathedral is a noble example, and when completed the work will add immensely to the beauty of that splendid, but formerly rather dingy pile; the parish church of Darlington possesses a reredos or altar-piece, consisting of a picture in mosaic on a large scale.

It has often been maintained that our somewhat damp climate, and the smoky atmosphere of our towns, form almost insurmountable barriers to the use of frescoes in modern England; but experiment seems to have proved the contrary. To name one or two cases in which this form of mural decoration has been successfully employed, reference may be made to the designs by the late Mr. Gambier Parry in Ely Cathedral, and paintings in St. Andrew's, Stoke Newington, St. John's, Isle of Dogs, St. Peter's, Bournemouth, St. Anne's, Derby, and elsewhere.

At Womersley, near Doncaster, is a curious picture in tiles, recently inserted in the south wall, the subject being the institution of the Eucharist. It is of foreign origin.

One set of pictures commonly found in Roman Catholic churches, and with increasing frequency in English ones, is the Stations of the Cross. As a rule these fourteen incidents in the Passion of the Saviour are treated in a way that, as art, is contemptible. Some few specimens, are however excellent; and when one remembers the dogmatic value of the facts set forth, and the pathos of that divine tragedy, one cannot but feel that art has here subjects worthy of its highest efforts. Antwerp Cathedral has a fine set of the Stations; and in England one of the best is at All Saint's, Scarborough.

On the continent we expect, of course, to find many excellent examples of paintings in churches, besides those altar-pieces and pictures to which allusion has already been made. Time has told its tale upon many examples, as on Leonardo da Vinci's "Last Supper," and neglect and carelessness are found there as well as at home, but actual violence has not been offered to ecclesiastical art abroad to the same extent as was the case in England. Time would fail, therefore, to discuss in any detail the instances that may be met with in continental churches. The works of Mrs. Jameson, and of others, have familiarized us all with many of the most important of them.

It will not be out of place to mention here a rather striking form of decoration employed in some continental cathedrals on great festivals. This consists of the display of large pictures worked in tapestry. At Rouen they are stretched around the columns in the nave, where besides their value as teachers, they add a useful warmth of colour to the place. At Brussels a similar custom prevails, but the tapestries, in this case framed, are hung between the pillars of the choir. In the choir at Aix, in Provence, are some tapestries stolen from St. Paul's by the Puritans, and sold in 1656.

In conclusion, the words of a layman on the use of pictures in churches are well worth quoting. "I should like to be told why a man may not look at a picture in church. Nobody wishes to put doing so in the place of attending to the service, or of listening to the sermon, even though the pictures be more eloquent and instructive. Why may not a man attend to all if he likes? Objections can only be based upon what may be called the *meeting-house* theory about churches; the theory that a church is intended to be used at certain specified times, and for public worship and preaching only, which ended, the congregation are to be turned out, and the place locked up till next 'service time.' . . . The parish church should be not only the place of public worship, but also the place of private meditation and prayer. Every parishoner should have free access to it at all reasonable times. Nay, it ought to be made interesting to attract him, and instructive to teach him when attracted." *

Such is surely common-sense, and is one more plea for the acceptance of the position, surely also common-sense, that the employment of art in all its forms, and in the highest degree attainable, is not a mere luxury, not a simple question of ornament, but a necessary element in the education of our race.

* Modern Parish Churches, by J. T. Micklethwaite, F.S.A., Architect, King & Co., 1874.

Flowers and the Rites of the Church.

By the Rev. Hilderic Friend.

THE sources of great rivers are often lost in the mists of far off mountains. It is thus with many popular usages. We may reasonably suppose that in the earliest and most distant ages man was wont to propitiate the object of his fear or worship by offering such things as were most pleasing to his own senses. Was he fond of flesh, the gods would share his tastes. Did he love fruit, so would they. Were fresh and fragrant flowers pleasing to his eye and sense, then the deity would find a similar pleasure in their use. Hence we find that in heathen lands the ceremonial use of flowers is practically universal. We also find flowers associated with present-day Buddhism, just as they were with the old time religions of Assyria and Egypt. The lotus was formerly, as it is even now, constantly associated in the East with religious rites, and anyone who is familiar with the temples of India and China, Burmah and Japan will recall the fact that the lotus-pool is one of their most frequent and indispensable adjuncts. And just as the lily and pomegranate found their way into the temple service and had their expressive symbolism, so in the Western church, represented by the Greek and Russian, Roman and English branches, numerous flowers have at different times been utilized.

It has been thought that after the Reformation and the Dissolution of monasteries, when the spirit of puritanism, and the reaction against excessive ritual prevailed, the ceremonial use of flowers fell into decay. Our records, however, rather tend to show that there was a revival of old-time usage in this respect during and after the time of Elizabeth. This is easily accounted for. The ritual of the church had firmly grasped the national sentiment. It had led to the multiplication of altars and vestments, of lights and ornaments, of symbols and ceremonies. The churches were rich in marketable goods. The plate, relics, and vestments, were of costly material, the gifts of the wealthy and the loyal, or of those who wished to expiate wrong ; and an impecunious exchequer could easily be enriched by the wholesale appropriation of such things under the pretence that they fostered superstition and idolatry. When, therefore, candles were forbidden, altars were cast down, chalice and pyx were confiscated, and gorgeous vestments were declared needless, a sense of baldness and coldness pervaded the sanctuary, and the heart yearned for some expression of emotion. Hence it is that we now find entries in the old account books for the purchase of flowers in the place of entries for candles and wax.

Thus, to give at present one example only; whereas the Churchwardens' Accounts for the Parish of St. Petrock, Exeter, up till the time of Elizabeth contain numberless entries relating to font tapers, candles called "Judas Candells," chrismatories, pyxes and holy water vessels, after that date we find instead entries "for bayes and flowres in the church," and "for roasemary and bays to be put aboute the church." From that time the usage has steadily grown, until it has come to be regarded, by conformist and nonconformist alike, as almost a necessity that at certain seasons of the year flowers should be employed.

I shall briefly sum up the uses of flowers in churches by reference to the occasions and manner of their use, and the kinds of flowers most in request, with the reasons for their selection.

The principal occasions upon which flowers have been employed in the church are three:—(1) the great church Festivals: Christmastide, Easter, and Whitsuntide; (2) the Dedication day, when special services were held in honour of the saint to whom the church owed its name; (3) other notable days, including May-day, Palm Sunday, Corpus Christi Day, St. Barnaby's Day, Trinity Sunday, the Day of St. John the Baptist, and others. That Christmastide should be a season of special rejoicing and consequent ritual cannot be a matter of surprise. Old books relating to church usages abound with proof that the season was one of unusual festivity, and while the home was enlivened with everything in the way of floral decoration which the season afforded, the church shared in the adornment. The account books of St. Mary-at-Hill, London, shew that, in 1486, fourpence was expended on " Holme and ivy at Christmas Eve." Holme was the old name for holly, from the Anglo-Saxon holen, but we must not suppose that the holly bush was so named because it was a holy plant. The churchwardens of St. Lawrence, Reading, in 1505, paid twopence "for the holy

FLOWERS AND RITES. 231

bush agayne Christmas," and similar disbursements are on record for many other churches. The practice of adorning the church with garlands and flowers was not, however, confined to Christmas. St. Martin, Outwick, supplies us with an entry to the effect that there was paid in 1524 " for brome agaynst Ester, 1d." The amount seems small, but its value was greater then than now. St.

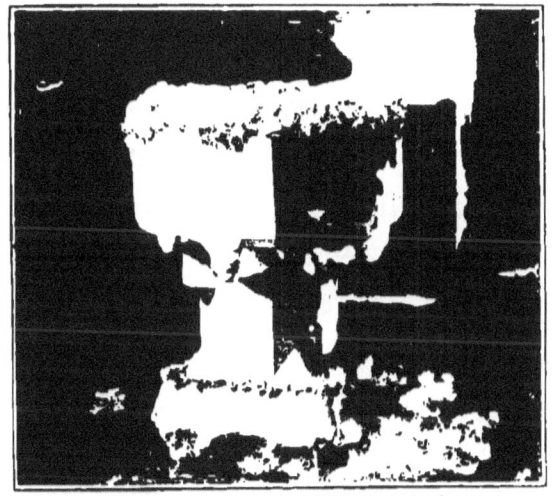

(From a photo. by Rev. Hilderic Friend).
OCTAGONAL FONT AT BOLTON, CUMBERLAND, WITH EASTER DECORATIONS.

Mary's Church, also in London, was more lavish. In one year the churchwardens paid, about this period, the sum of 3s. for three great garlands made of roses and lavender for the crosses, and three dozen other garlands for the choir, for the Easter decorations.

Whitsuntide was also one of the seasons of special rejoicing. The stitchwort (*Stellaria holostea*) has sometimes been spoken of as the special flower of this season, and its local names in different parts of the country seem to indicate as much. I have reason, however, to believe that it is rather to be associated with White Sunday—the day on which the candidates (those who were adorned with white raiment, symbolic of purity) were required to appear in church. We may remind our readers that a brief account of the day may be found, with much other useful information bearing on this theme, in Brand's *Popular Antiquities*. Numerous entries are found in old records relating to garlands at Whitsuntide, while in more than one county benefactors left a plot of ground that the grass might be mown for strewing the church at this season of the year. The custom of strewing rushes has been frequently alluded to, but does not come within the scope of my present essay.

The custom of decorating the church on dedication day is well established. As each church has its own patron saint or saints it will readily be seen that there is scarcely a day in the year when some sanctuary or other is not made bright with floral garniture. Such events, however, are of purely local interest. We may therefore pass by this to notice a few of the other events on which the use of flowers was required. On Palm Sunday the triumphal entry into Jerusalem is celebrated, and since the palm is not an English tree other plants have been pressed into service. A dictionary of plant names will show that many other shrubs besides the willow are locally known as palms. The willow, however, from its general prevalence, as well as from the fact that its catkins are usually in their prime about this season, "bears the palm." In 1536 we find it recommended, among other things, that "vestments for God's service, holy water, candles on Candlemas Day, palms on Palm Sunday, and other laudable customs" be continued in the church. In 1548 we read that "the ceremony of bearing palmes on Palme Sunday was left off, and not used as before." The people, however, were loth to give up their old usage, and between 1630 and 1640 enquiry was to be made by authority whether there be any superstitious use of crosses, palms, or other memories of idolaters. In some Roman Catholic countries it is still customary to employ sprigs of boxwood for palms on this occasion. It was so formerly in England, while yew, myrtle, and olive have also here and elsewhere found place. At the beginning of the sixteenth century we find several churches, including All Hallows, Staining, and St. Martin, Outwich, London, entering accounts for "palme and box flowers" or "flowers and yow"; also "Item for box and palme on Palme Sunday; Item for gennepore (juniper) for the church, 2d."

On St. John the Baptist's Day many floral rites were observed. The sun was now at its zenith of splendour, and John was "a burning and shining light." St. John's wort is still the popular name for one genus of plants (*Hypericum*) which blossom at this season, and have a truly solar appearance. Then there was Corpus Christi Day—a festival widely observed. Thereon the churches were nicely decorated; flags were brought forth, torches were garnished with flowers, and garlands were lavishly employed. It must have cost some of our churches a large sum annually in the days when flowers were regularly purchased for these and similar uses. To-day the tendency is for loving hands to render voluntary service, while in some sanctuaries a special box is placed near the main entrance, clearly described as a receptacle for offerings to be used in the purchase of flowers for regular use on the altar, or for periodical decoration. Among the many other occasions to which reference might be made, perhaps St. Barnaby's Day is the most noteworthy. The reason is that June 11th, the day on which S. Barnabas is held in honour, represents that period of the year when the day is longest and the night is shortest :—

" . . . . Barnaby bright,
The longest day and shortest night."

Hence we read of " Rose garlands and lavender for St. Barnabas, 1s. 6d.," and " For rose garlandis and Woodrove garlandis on St. Barnebe's Day, 11d." Also " Item. for 2 doss. de bocse garlands for prestes and clerkes on St. Barnebe's Daye, 1s. 10d."

This latter entry suggests an enquiry into the modes of use. Flowers were lavishly and frequently employed, but in what manner were they disposed, or to what uses were they put? It would be utterly impossible in a single chapter to answer this question in detail. Naturally the altar has always claimed first attention. The accounts of the steward of the Corpus Christi Guild, Leicester, contain the following entry for the year 1525-6:—" Item for garnyshing off the awter, iiis. iiiid." This custom of adorning the altar is now in some churches perpetual rather than occasional. The rood-loft was also decorated. We are told that "At Charlton-on-Otmoor, in Oxfordshire, there is a rood-loft of finely-carved oak, probably of the time of Henry the Seventh, upon which the original colour and gilding is yet to be seen. On this rood-loft it is the custom to place a garland, formed upon a large wooden cross, on May-day; which garland remains there until the following year, when it is renewed with fresh flowers and leaves, occupying the position of the ancient Holy Rood of former ages. It was formerly the custom to carry this cross in procession round the village before finally depositing it in its resting-place in the church." I have already adduced evidence that the cross was garlanded at Easter with wreaths made of roses, lavender, and other sweet herbs. In the old-time church there were frequently numerous crosses of various sizes belonging to one edifice. Some of these stood on the altars which were also numerous; one or more occupied the rood-loft, while yet others were carried in procession. This will be clearly gathered from a brief inspection of the inventories of church goods, compiled in the time of Edward

VI., as well as from other official records. Then we have "garlands for the choir," or quire, decorations for pews and pillars, wreaths for suspending from the walls, deckings for the torches, and, by no means least noteworthy, garlands for the priests. From Polydore Vergil and others we learn that formerly, not only was it customary to decorate the church with flowers, but the priests also performed the service, on certain high days, crowned with flowers. This was notably the case at St. Paul's Cathedral, London, and more particularly on the feast-day of the patron saint. At St. Mary's, in 1486, the sum of 1s. 10d. was paid for two dozen garlands of box for the priests and clerks on St. Barnabas' Day, and frequent items are found in other accounts of a similar character. We shall recall the action of the priests of Lycaonia, who brought garlands and oxen with which to celebrate their worship.

It remains to say a word respecting the flowers employed or tabooed on these festive occasions. Individual preferences might go for something, the season of the year regulated many things, while religious and old-time associations did the rest. Some flowers have, by universal consent, been regarded as peculiarly appropriate for ceremonial uses. The daffodil appearing just at the season of Lent, naturally lends itself to the church decorator. Holly and ivy must of necessity be in special request at Christmastide, the rose has always been regarded as seasonable, whenever it could be obtained, while the lily is universally typical of the Virgin. Lavender and bay are sweet and fragrant. St. John's wort comes just at the right season for celebrating the saint whose name it bears, the hellebore, or winter rose, is significant of, and dedicated to St. Agnes, and comes at a season when flowers are rare. Purity is well represented by the snowdrop, the passion-flower (though a modern introduction) has readily taken hold of English feeling and sentiment, the willow serves for Palm Sunday, while the innocent and beautiful blossoms of the primrose and woodruffe, the fragrant flowers of the violet, and the showy compound heads of the marigold, each present their own features of attractiveness. There are not many flowers which come amiss. A few are excluded on account of their disagreeable odour, and it is believed that the mistletoe has been generally tabooed on account of its heathen associations, though its name is frequently introduced into the doggerel of the past two centuries as one of the plants employed in church decorations at Christmas.

The ceremonial use of flowers has of recent

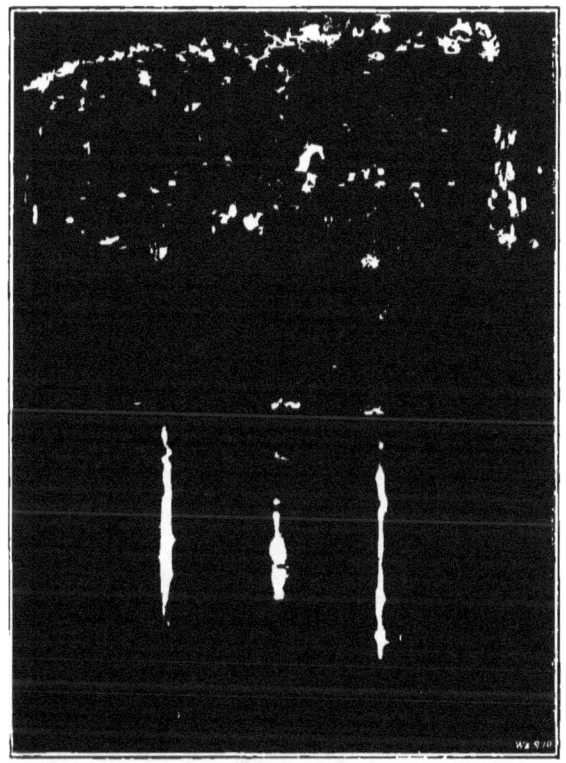

(From a photo. by Rev. Hilderic Friend).
ROMAN FONT AT CROSS CANONBY, CUMBERLAND, WITH EASTER DECORATIONS.

years greatly revived. In village, town, and city the ancient or modern sanctuary may be seen at frequent intervals from New Year to Christmas brightened with blossoms or decorated with evergreens, while in many cases the altar is daily adorned with fresh flowers whenever they can be obtained. At Easter especially, when the anemone and blue-bell, the primrose and violet are in profusion, font and altar, pillar and pew are frequently covered with a lavish profusion of flower and foliage, and last year as I went the round of a number of village churches in Lakeland I was able to take numerous photographs of fonts and chancels thus adorned. The two illustrations supplied herewith are samples of what may be seen.

It has well been said that of all customs, that of adorning the "Holy Place of the tabernacle of the most High" with flowers and wreaths at Christmas and other festivals of the Christian year, "speaks of the simple faith and fervent love of our ancestors, more strongly than any other," at those times of the year when the beauties of nature prompted men to look up "From Nature unto Nature's God," and we trust the usage will long continue as a tribute of love and devotion.

Ghost-Layers and Ghost-Laying.

By the Rev. R. Wilkins Rees.

INCREDIBLE though it may seem it is none the less true, that a canon authorising exorcism under episcopal licence is still a part of the ecclesiastical law of the Anglican church. The writer does not suppose, however, that any present occupant of the episcopal bench has received an application for a faculty, notwithstanding the fact that we live in an age of Mahatmas, second-sight, visions, clairvoyance, astral planes, and other wonders.

One of the most interesting descriptions of ghost-laying is supplied by "An Account of an Apparition, attested by the Rev. William Rudall, Minister at Launceston, in Cornwall," written in 1665. But before extended reference is made to the strange experiences therein alluded to, the concluding paragraph of the account shall be given in full:—" To the ignorance of men in our age in this particular and mysterious part of philosophy and religion—namely, the communication between spirits and men—not one scholar out of ten thousand, though otherwise of excellent learning, knows anything of it, or the way how to manage it. This ignorance breeds fear and abhorrence of that which otherwise might be of incomparable benefit to mankind."

G. S. Gilbert, in his "Historical Survey of Cornwall," refers at length to Rudall's story, but the extremely fascinating narrative, "The Botathen Ghost," from the versatile pen of the late Rev. R. S. Hawker, Morwenstow, is unquestionably the best account of all. It would seem that Parson Rudall's "Diurnal" fell by chance into Mr. Hawker's hands, and it is hardly possible to imagine that the manuscript could have received more skilful treatment or more sympathetic attention. The unusual character of Rudall's "Diurnal," together with the particulars it contains in connection with ghost-laying, will be adequate excuse for what, otherwise, might be considered undue quotation.

"A singular infelicity," says the learned Launceston parson, "had befallen young Master Bligh, once the hopeful heir of his parents and of the lands of Botathen. Whereas he had been from childhood a blithe and merry boy, 'the gladness,' like Isaac of old, of his father's age, he had suddenly, and of late, become morose and silent—nay, even austere and stern—dwelling apart, always solemn, often in tears," but at last he disclosed the secret cause—that he was haunted by the spirit of one Dorothy Dinglet. At the urgent request of his friends and a resident clergyman the lad made a confidant of Parson Rudall, and eventually went with him to the field—still pointed out—where he was in the habit of meeting the apparition. Rudall himself there saw the ghostly visitor, and on returning to the house promised the boy and his parents that, when he had fulfilled certain business elsewhere, he would come back and take orders to assuage the disturbances and their cause.

The diary thus proceeds: "January 7, 1665.—At my own house, I find, by my books, what is expedient to be done; and then, *Apage Sathanas!*

"January 9, 1665.—This day I took leave of my wife and family, under pretext of engagements elsewhere, and made my secret journey to our diocesan city, wherein the good and venerable bishop then abode.

"January 10.—*Deo gratias*, in safe arrival at

Exeter; craved and obtained immediate audience of his lordship; pleading it was for counsel and admonition on a weighty and pressing cause; called to the presence; made obeisance; and then by command stated my case—the Botathen perplexity—which I moved with strong and earnest instances and solemn asseverations of that which I had myself seen and heard. Demanded by his lordship, what was the succour that I had come to entreat at his hands? Replied, licence for my exorcism, that so I might, ministerially, allay this spiritual visitant, and thus render to the living and the dead release from this surprise. 'But,' said our bishop, 'on what authority do you allege that I am intrusted with faculty so to do? Our Church, as is well known, hath abjured certain branches of her ancient power, on grounds of perversion and abuse.' 'Nay, my lord,' I humbly answered, 'under favour, the seventy-second of the canons ratified and enjoined on us, the clergy, anno Domino 1604, doth expressly provide, that: "No minister, unless he hath the licence of his diocesan bishop, shall essay to exorcise a spirit, evil or good." Therefore it was, I did here mildly allege, 'that I did not presume to enter on such a work without lawful privilege under your lordship's hand and seal.' Hereupon did our wise and learned bishop, sitting in his chair, condescend upon the theme at some length with many gracious interpretations from ancient writers and from Holy Scripture, and I did humbly rejoin and reply, till the upshot was that he did call in his secretary, and command him to draw the aforesaid faculty, forthwith and without further delay, assigning him a form, insomuch that the matter was incontinently done; and after I had disbursed into the secretary's hands certain moneys for signitary purposes, as the manner of such officers hath always been, the bishop did himself affix his signature under the *sigillum* of his see, and deliver the document into my hands. When I knelt down to receive his benediction, he softly said, 'Let it be secret, Mr. R. Weak brethren! weak brethren!'

"January 11, 1665.—Therewithal did I hasten home and prepare my instruments, and cast my figures for the onset of the next day. Took out my ring of brass and put it on the index-finger of my right hand, with the *scutum Davidis* traced thereon.

"January 12, 1665.—Rode into the gateway at Botathen, armed at all points, but not with Saul's armour, and ready. There is danger from the demons, but so there is in the surrounding air every day. At early morning then, and alone, —for so the usage ordains,—I betook me towards the field. It was void, and I had thereby due time to prepare. First, I paced and measured out my circle on the grass. Then did I mark my pentacle in the very midst, and at the intersection of the five angles I did set up and fix my crutch of *raun* (rowan). Lastly, I took my station south, at the true line of the meridian, and stood facing due north. I waited and watched for a long time. At last there was a kind of trouble in the air, a soft and rippling sound, and all at once the shape appeared, and came on towards me gradually. I opened my parchment-scroll and read aloud the command. She paused, and seemed to waver and doubt; stood still; then I rehearsed the sentence again, sounding out every syllable like a chant. She drew near my ring, but halted at first outside, on the brink. I sounded again, and now at the third time I gave the signal in Syriac—the speech which is used, they say, where such ones dwell and converse in thoughts that glide.

"She was at last obedient, and swam into

the midst of the circle, and there stood still, suddenly. I saw, moreover, that she drew back her pointing hand. All this while I do confess that my knees shook under me, and the drops of sweat ran down my flesh like rain. But now, although face to face with the spirit, my heart grew calm, and my mind was composed. I knew that the pentacle would govern her, and the ring must bind, until I gave the word. Then I called to mind the rule laid down of old, that no angel or fiend, no spirit, good or evil, will ever speak until they have been first spoken to. N.B.— This is the great law of prayer. God Himself will not yield reply until man hath made vocal entreaty, once and again. So I went on to demand, as the books advise, and the phantom made answer, willingly. Questioned wherefore not at rest? Unquiet, because of a certain sin. Asked why, and by whom? Revealed it; but it is *sub sigillo*, and therefore *nefas dictu*; more anon. Inquired, what sign she could give that she was a true spirit and not a false fiend? Stated, before next Yule-tide a fearful pestilence would lay waste the land, and myriads of souls would be loosened from their flesh, until, as she piteously said, 'our valleys will be full.' Asked again, why she so terrified the lad? Replied: 'It is the law; we must seek a youth or a maiden of clean life, and under age, to receive messages and admonitions.' We conversed with many more words, but it is not lawful for me to set them down. Pen and ink would degrade and defile the thoughts she uttered, and which my mind received that day. I broke the ring, and she passed, but to return once more next day. At even-song, a long discourse with that ancient transgressor, Mr. B. Great horror and remorse; entire atonement and penance; whatsoever I enjoin; full acknowledgment before pardon.

"January 13, 1665.—At sunrise I was again in the field. She came in at once, and, as it seemed, with freedom. Inquired if she knew my thoughts, and what I was going to relate? Answered, 'Nay, we only know what we perceive and hear; we cannot see the heart.' Then I rehearsed the penitent words of the man she had come up to denounce, and the satisfaction he would perform. Then said she, 'Peace in our midst.' I went through the proper forms of dismissal, and fulfilled all as it was set down and written in my memoranda; and then, with certain fixed rites, I did dismiss that troubled ghost, until she peacefully withdrew, gliding towards the west. Neither did she ever afterward appear, but was allayed until she shall come in her second flesh to the valley of Armageddon on the last day."

One further entry in Rudall's "Diurnal," under date July 10, 1665, must be given : "How sorely must the infidels and heretics of this generation be dismayed when they know that this black death (*i.e.* the Great Plague), which is now swallowing its thousands in the streets of the great city, was foretold six months agone, under the exorcisms of a country minister, by a visible and suppliant ghost!"

Of the apparent sincerity of this record there can be little doubt, and the facts contained in it are referred to with, at least, a certain amount of credence even to the present day. But Parson Rudall's narrative of the Botathen ghost by no means exhausts the ghost-laying stories of the south-west of England, and in the remaining part of this chapter a selection is given indicating various methods and connected with various localities.

All tourists to the Lizard district will remember Mullion church, if but for the superior carvings—

quaintly and diversely designed—which adorn its ancient benches. In the chancel is a tablet to the memory of Thomas Flavel, a former vicar of the parish, who died in 1682, and on the brass immediately beneath it is the curious inscription:

> "Earth, take thine Earth, my Sin let Satan havet.
> The World my goods; my Soul my God who gavet;
> For from these four—Earth, Satan, World, and God—
> My flesh, my Sin, my goods, my Soul, I had."

Flavel was credited with possessing to a remarkable degree the power of "laying" ghosts, and all advances in intelligence have utterly failed to throw discredit on his marvellous skill or the stories told in connection with its exorcise. One morning when Flavel was engaged in the service at church, a prying servant entered his sanctum, and incautiously opening a book on the black-art, raised at once a legion of evil spirits. Through his power of second-sight the parson became aware of this as he was reading the prayers. He abruptly closed the service, and returned in haste to the vicarage. There he found the poor servant still in the study, distracted with fear and tormented by the spirits. Quickly seizing the book, Flavel proceeded to read backwards the passages at which the girl had glanced, all the while striking in every direction with the stout walking-stick that he carried. The spirits were soon dismissed, but not before they had so abused the servant that for days she bore evidences of their violence!

These extraordinary powers caused Flavel to be summoned to the aid of many far and near. On one occasion he was called to settle a ghost that for long had baffled and defied all other skill, and no less a sum than five guineas was required by him as payment for the "laying" of this unruly spirit. Because of such an expenditure, two men interested in the matter thought that the exorcist should be watched so that they might be satisfied as to the performance of his task. Neither, however, made a confidant of the other, and on the night of the ceremony they were posted behind different gravestones, each wholly unconscious of the presence of his friend. At the appointed hour Flavel arrived, armed with a heavy whip and a book of divination. Crack went the whip, and both the spies started in fear! Each caught sight of the frightened face of the other, and in dread alarm at what seemed a ghostly appearance ran as though for life, leaving the vicar to settle accounts in his own fashion with the spirit. When Flavel died his ghost was "laid" by a clergyman of whom he had said, "When he comes I must go." The exact spot where this was done is even now indicated.

Scarcely five miles distant from the celebrated well of St. Keyne is the village of Talland, known for its picturesquely situated church with detached tower. This church is said to owe its present position, as do other Cornish churches, such as Lelant, Mawgan, and Gunwalloe, to the fact that every night the devil removed the stones that had been elsewhere placed by day. Night after night a mysterious voice came :—

"If you will my wish fulfil,
Build the church on Talland hill."

But about a hundred and fifty years ago his satanic majesty met his match in the Talland vicar, the Rev. Richard Dodge, whose authority over the spirit world was simply supreme. With him the slightest effort of the will sufficed to raise or "lay" the inhabitants of the other world, and a nod of the head to send any troublesome ghost to that safest of all spirit-prisons, the depths of the Red Sea. His people held him in the deepest dread, and all shrank from any nightly encounter with one who, in the hours of darkness, would be preceded, almost invariably, by a host of evil spirits whom, with unsparing hand, he would be driving before him.

For years the horrible apparition of a funeral coach drawn by headless horses had terrified the people of Lanreath, a neighbouring parish, where it would be often seen crossing Blackadown moor at a fiendlike pace. At last the Lanreath parson implored the aid of his brother Dodge, and at the dead of night they rode to the haunted spot. Nothing, however, was to be seen, and after a while the clergymen separated, each turning towards home. But no great distance had Dodge gone when his horse, with the preternatural sight its tribe is often declared to possess, stood stockstill, refusing to take another step in the direction of Talland. "This," thought he, "must surely be a sign from heaven," and throwing the reins on the horse's neck he permitted the animal to go as it chose. Back to the haunted moor it went, and there in the gloom could be perceived at last the dark forms of the funeral coach and its headless horses. The driver had descended from his seat and was standing in a threatening attitude over the prostrate body of the Lanreath vicar lying as if dead at the spectre's feet. Such a sight was enough to shatter even the iron nerve of Parson Dodge; but, notwithstanding all alarm, the sense of duty so possessed him that he quickly began the words of exorcism. Before the prayer, short though it was, could be ended, the phantom coachman started, exclaiming, "Dodge is come, I must be gone," and, springing to his box, drove the phantom team away like the wind, and nevermore returned. But, though Dodge's ghost-laying was most effectual, days elapsed before the Lanreath vicar regained his senses.

The late William Bottrell ("An Old Celt"), that indefatigable collector of the traditions and hearthside stories of Cornwall, tells an extraordinary story of ghost-laying, the scene of which is laid at Bosava near Lamorna. The devil, in the capacity of a master-mason, had materially helped a miserly old cobbler to build a fine house, and had bargained with him for the surrender of his life after a certain period. But the cobbler tricked the devil, and as a consequence, even after the death of the former, such a war was waged between the two that a miller who lived near the haunted house, on which no roof could ever be securely fixed, fared badly both in person and in pocket. The miller ultimately begged Parson Corker, a noted huntsman, ghost-layer, and devil-driver, who lived in the neighbourhood, to exert his power on the devil and cobbler. "He thought that if the parson could not succeed in driving them away, he might at least, as he was a justice, bind them over to keep the peace."

"After the parson and his friends had well fortified themselves, as well as the miller, with plenty of strong drink (that they might be the better able to undertake the difficult work), they all started about midnight from the parson's plaisance for the scene of their ghostly operations, and arrived at Bosava in the small hours of the morning.

"They say that when the parson, assisted by Dr. Maddern and the miller, drew the magic pentagram and sacred triangle, within which they placed themselves for safety, and commenced the other ceremonies, only known to the learned, which are required for the effectual subjugation of restless spirits, an awful gale sprang up in the cove (Lamorna) and raged up the vale with increasing fury, until scarcely a tree was left standing in the bottom. Yet there was scarcely a breath of wind stirring in other places. As the parson continued to read, the devil swore, howled, shrieked, and roared louder than the raging storm. The parson, undaunted, read on and performed more powerful operations in the art of exorcism, till the sweat boiled from his body so that there was not a dry thread on him, and he was beginning to fear that he had met with more than his match, when the whole force of the storm gathered itself around the haunted house, and the tree to which the parson clung, that he might not be blown away, was rooted from the ground, and swept by the gale, parson and all, right across the water. Then the thatch, timbers, and stones were seen, by the lightning flashes, to fly all over the bottom. One of the sharp spars from the thatch stuck in the parson's side, and made a wound which pained him ever after. Yet, not to be baffled, the parson made the black spirit hear spells that were stronger still. A moment after the devil (as if in defiance of the parson) had made a clean sweep of the roof, from amidst the wreck of the building a figure was seen to rise in the shape of the dark master-mason, and fly away in the black thunder cloud, with his level, square, plumb-line, compasses, and other tools around him.

"After the devil had disappeared there was a lull in the tempest. The brave parson then tried his power on the cobbler, who might still be heard beating his lapstone louder than ever. The parson, after summoning him to appear, and after much trouble in chasing the obstinate spirit of the old miser from place to place, at last caught him in the pulrose under the mill-wheel. Then the ghost threw his hammer and lapstone at the parson's head, at the same time crying out, 'Now, Corker, that thee art come I must be gone, but it's only for a time.' Luckily the parson was too well acquainted with spiritual weapons to let ghostly tools do him any harm. The night was passed. The parson's power had compelled both demon and cobbler to depart. After making a wreck of the house between them, the parson could do no more for the miller. But a few days after it was found that the old cobbler had returned to the charge, making more noise and annoyance about the place than ever, by broad daylight even as bad as by night, and that the parson could only hunt him from spot to spot about the wreck of the haunted place, without being able to make the noises cease from amidst the ruins. It was then decided to demolish all the walls of the devil's building.

"There the best piece of work ever seen in this part of the country was long ago destroyed, and the stones employed for building hedges and out-houses. No one cared to use them about any dwelling-house, for fear that the old miserly cobbler might claim them and again settle down to beat his lapstone beside them."

Such is one of the most extreme and fanciful of those stories of the supernatural which Cornish people are wont to relate earnestly even to this day.

Near Grampound Road Station on the Great Western Railway, and not far from Truro, is the parish of Ladock where lived, about a century since, another ghost-laying parson of undoubted powers. Mr. Woods, this master of spirits, generally used as a walking-stick a staff made of ebony, and having a strange silver head embellished with a five-sided figure of mystic import, and a silver band bearing the signs of the zodiac and various hieroglyphics. Parson Woods usually dealt with obnoxious spirits in a summary fashion. By some magic rite he made them incarnate in the form of any brute he might fancy, and then gave them an unmerciful horsewhipping. But on one occasion he was set at nought by a spirit who, with demoniacal cunning, took the shape of a bird of sombre hue and strange appearance, which most frequently occupied a position in the belfry where, during the conduct of divine service, it would make all kinds of ludicrous noises, to the chagrin of the vicar, the annoyance of the devout, and the delight of the young and irreverent. There was no possibility of administering a thrashing to the bird, and the spirit was much too far away to be properly "laid." At last the poor clergyman, driven almost to despair, was made aware of the fact that no evil spirit could remain in any locality after being brought face to face with innocent children, and all parents in the parish having unbaptised children were at once urged to bring their youngsters to the church on the next Sunday to be christened. Eight children were thus to be brought, but as the charm could only work effectually when twelve, the prescribed number, were present, four mothers whose babies had been recently baptised were requested to bring their children also. The eight infants were duly christened; and then in solemn procession the vicar and the mothers with the children and their sponsors left the church. Opposite the belfry door the procession stopped, and the parson directed each mother to hand her child to its sponsor who in turn was to pass it to him so that he might hold it out for the demon to see. But the crafty bird remained hidden at the top of the tower, and no effort availed to dislodge it from behind the pinnacles. Luckily some of the babies began to cry, and soon, as a natural result, there was a perfect babel of infant voices. This proved too much even for the curiosity of a demon, and unthinkingly the bird hopped out from its hiding-place to see what could have occurred. The sight of the twelve children at once cast the desired spell, and with a screaming noise, louder and more hideous than that produced by the dozen children, the bird took to its wings and disappeared, never again troubling the church, its precincts, or the neighbourhood.

But no mention of the ghost-laying parsons of the Delectable Duchy can be considered complete without the inclusion of the Rev. Mr. Jago, a famous vicar of Wendron, near Helston. Of Jago it was said that, though he used to ride far and wide over the moorland of his parish, he never took a groom with him, for the moment he alighted from his horse he had but to strike the earth with his whip to summon a demon-groom to take charge of his steed. At certain cross-roads, about a quarter of a mile from Wendron Church-town, the place is pointed out where Jago "laid" the ghost of a poor suicide who had been buried there. It was supposed that no spirit walking the earth could resist the spells of this mighty parson, and that he could even make ghosts appear as marks of delicate attention to those who might be walking with him! From him many a night-wanderer has received his quietus, and all the people of his time seem to have been strangely impressed by his tremendous powers. The tradition remains that to all the evil-disposed he was also a constant terror, for it was firmly believed that every act was visible to him at the moment it was done—whether at night or in the day. Consequently he could indicate criminals with unerring directness, and those who before had never been suspected confessed at once to deeds of wrong when brought under the lightning glance of Jago's eye.

We should hardly expect to find John Wesley among the list of ghost-layers, and there is no doubt that his supposed encounter with spirits at St. Agnes is known to very few. Not one of the lives of the great religious leader alludes to it, while Jeffrey's ghost at Epworth parsonage is usually given a place of honour. The story runs that, during one of his frequent journeys through Cornwall, Wesley was compelled when visiting St. Agnes to spend the night in a house which was declared to be possessed by evil spirits. Nothing daunted, the brave little man retired to bed, but soon his rest was broken by loud and angry sounds below. Now the roll of carriage wheels could be distinctly heard, then the tramp of feet,—all to be succeeded by blasphemy and curses. Wesley speedily left his bed, and hurrying to the rooms beneath his chamber found a large number of people seated about the table in the hall. Boisterous words of welcome hailed his appearance, and the good man was jovially requested to join them at their merry meal. "Yes," said he, "but I must say grace first." The building rang with the laughter with which these words were greeted, but with unmoved courage Wesley broke in with the line, "Jesus, the Name high over all." Instantly the lights disappeared; utter darkness prevailed; not a sign was to be seen; not a voice was to be heard; and for ever after the house was freed from its ghostly terrors.

The parson's presence has been considered

indispensable in all ghost-laying operations, but the following story, related in all good faith to the writer by those who received it from the woman in question and her praying friends, would throw discredit on the *absolute* necessity of clerical aid. Not many miles from Penzance is a little village called after its church, supposed to be dedicated to St. Swithin, near which stands a cottage—the scene some years ago of a strange occurrence. Here lived a woman of striking appearance, who, in deference to friends still living, shall be called Johanna Johns. For long she had worked in the service of a farmer and his wife whose immediate descendants now live in the old homestead, and when the master died he left her a substantial annuity, to be paid after the decease of her mistress. The farmer's widow, in her last hours, implored Johanna to take all possible care of a favourite dog, but notwithstanding the servant's repeated promise to fulfil her mistress's wish, the poor brute was shamefully neglected, and as a consequence very soon died.

Thenceforward Johanna was haunted without intermission by the spirit of her mistress, and vain were all attempts to "lay" the intruder. But at last the ghost so far relented as to inform the woman that it would be quieted, but that she alone should accomplish the feat; and that when a few days had elapsed she must be prepared to proceed to the churchyard at midnight for the purpose. Deliverance was cheap, however, to any price.

The eventful night came. Johanna sat near her kitchen window with a pious Methodist on either side praying earnestly in her behalf. Suddenly, at the stroke of twelve, a strange wind seemed to sweep right through the room, and when the men lifted their heads the woman was gone! About an hour elapsed; and then, with awed and pallor-stricken face, she returned to relate the eventful experience of that brief space of time. The ghost had indeed come for her, and she was borne without the house, when she distinctly heard the words breathed into her ear, "Over or under?" Hardly knowing what she said, she gasped "Over," and straightway was carried far above the earth. Up, up she went, beyond the church's lofty tower, and then right on towards the east. Soon, in the weird light that seemed to be diffused abroad, she distinctly discerned beneath her the tall, gaunt trees surrounding an old and famous house about two miles distant from her home. Then the course was changed to the north, and speedily she was flying over the low, straggling houses of the village on a neighbouring hill. Once more the course was changed, and now to the south-west—homewards. Together the spirit and Johanna descended into the churchyard and approached the grave at whose head stood the stone bearing the name of the dead mistress—they drew near to the grave of the ghost! Here the "laying" of the spirit was successfully accomplished, and the woman returned to her cottage once more free from the haunting presence. "But what was done at the graveside?" eagerly demanded the men who had been praying with her. The only response to this question was a fit of agonised crying. The secret of the graveside rites she was not permitted to reveal, and to her dying day she kept it safe. Again and again curious neighbours and people from a distance came to hear the queer, unearthly story, but when they endeavoured to wrest from her this part of her experience the only response was that evoked by the memories of the awful night—an outburst of bitter tears. Such is a story accepted as unquestionably true by those who, perhaps, were best able to judge of its veracity. For a long time previous to her death, Johanna was esteemed as a good and devout woman, but to her last days she solemnly declared that her story was nothing more than a narration of indisputable fact. Let the unbeliever, therefore, make of it what he will.

The clergyman was supposed to conduct the ghost-laying ceremony, as a rule, in Latin, a language that struck the most audacious spirit in all the world with terror. The penalties imposed by the ghost-layer were various. The ghost of Mrs. Baines, which haunted Chapel Street, Penzance, was bound by a powerful exorcist, Parson Singleton, to spin ropes of sand from the banks on the western green for a term of a thousand years, unless she, before that time, spun a rope sufficiently long and strong to reach from St. Michael's Mount to St. Clement's Isle. Some knowing ones have asserted that generally these obstreperous ghosts might be laid for any term less than a hundred years, and in any place or body, full or empty, which was very convenient; as, for instance, a solid oak, or the pommel of a sword, or a barrel of beer, if a farmer or simple gentleman, or a butt of wine, if a county magistrate, a big squire, or a lord. But of all places, as it has been already hinted, that which a ghost least liked was the Red Sea; it being related that ghosts have prayed their exorcists not to continue them in that place. It was nevertheless considered an incontestable fact that there was an infinite number laid there, perhaps from its being, somehow, a safer prison than any other nearer at hand; though neither history nor tradition gives us any instance of ghosts escaping or returning from this kind of transportation before their time. About the year 1761, a pinnacle was thrown down by lightning from the tower of the church at Ludgvan. The effect was then universally imputed, so Mr. Robert Hunt tells us, to the vengeance of a perturbed spirit, exorcised from Treassow, and passing eastward, towards the usual place of banishment—the Red Sea.

Even in these days the clergy are not supposed to have lost this power over the spirit world, and quite recently there have been cases in which they were implored to exercise it. The writer has it on good authority that a poor woman living, at any rate till recently, in Madron near Penzance, went not long ago to the house of a clergyman residing there, and asked him to walk round her, reading some passages from the Bible to exorcise the ghost of her dead sister who had entered into her, she said, and was tormenting her in the shape of a small fly which continually buzzed in her ear. Once, when before the Board of Guardians, she talked sensibly for a time, then suddenly stopped and exclaimed, shaking her head as she did so, " Be quiet, you brute! don't you see I'm talking to the gentleman?"

Church Walks.

By the Rev. W. B. Russell Caley, M.A., F.R.H.S.

WHEN the parish church had been built, either by the munificence of some landowner, or through the laudable wish of a neighbouring monastic establishment to provide for the spiritual necessities of the country population, the first question that arose was "How to get to it?" If it was not by a road this was no easy problem to solve. Often must the villagers in winter have looked across at their church and seen "a morass" between them and it, or else a wild and rugged common. Now it is the birthright of every Englishman to be able to get to his parish church, so "a way" to it was a necessity, unless the said church was in the midst of the village, or abutting on the high road. From this manifest need arose "Church Walks," or as we find them in towns, "Church Alleys" (probably in days long ago—brier-hung lanes—gay with many-coloured flowers, before the town absorbed the country). The landowner having built the church near his own dwelling, in most cases, would grant the people leave to cross his land to come to church, or they would take "French leave," generally, as a matter of course, choosing the direct line from the village to the church. Then underwood must be cut away, and holes filled up, and mounds levelled, till a regular track was made; this, in time, became a recognized "right of way," or the "Church Walk." But human nature is not soon satisfied. It must have been unpleasant to run the gauntlet of stray cattle, etc., on the way to church, an unruly horse, or a vicious bull must have been a severe trial to the faith and courage of some would-be worshippers, so the churchwardens, prompted by the vestry, would consider the advisability of putting up fences, and the weaker members of the community rejoiced. Yet, although the hedges afforded protection from wandering quadrupeds, and gave shelter from wintry blasts, they did not protect from the noon-day sun. Trees must be planted; the leafy shelter made church-going a pleasure, and young lovers delighted in the welcome shade on moonlight nights.

The Church Walk became the pride of the village. The pleasant avenue, with the old grey church standing in its framework of green at the end, was the greatest charm of the place. Old folks ambled there, young folk sauntered there, children romped there. The more serious minded of the parish would not be satisfied with this.

IN THE PARISH STOCKS, BY ALFRED CROWQUILL.

Why not place before the eyes of those who used this "Walk," object lessons in morality? This surely was the place for the parish stocks. So "the Stocks" stood there, and persons going to the House of God saw many sad instances of the sorrow and sin that results from breaking His commandments, while the unfortunates in the stocks, being the subject of the pity or scorn of the parish, learnt that the way of transgressors is hard.

These "Church Walks" were seldom, or never, used for wheeled traffic, by ancient custom they were only Bridle-paths, or foot-paths, and in later years gates have usually been placed at the end, or ends, to prevent an infringement of this wise regulation; neither was any owner, or tenant of adjoining land, allowed to break through the hedges and erect gates. The churchwardens maintained the "Walk" in repair at the cost of the church lands (if there were any), or church rates. But all these things are passing away with other "Bygones." Church rates vanished, and with them church revenues got so low that the "wardens" were glad to let the keeping up drop into the hands of the Parish Surveyor and the rates. Private interest prevailed over the public weal, and on the "give and take" principle, some persons were allowed to make gates and cart up the Walk on to their lands; while the grand old trees that had sheltered so many generations of parishioners, being considered too shady for the neighbouring soil, have been cut down. Thus the old Church Walks of our land are gradually, but surely, losing their distinctive features, and will soon, under the dominion and intrigues of Parish Councils, become only a memory of the past.

Shakespeare possibly alluded to such "Walks" when he said, "The why is plain as way to parish church," for in his days these ways would be almost in their prime. Nothing perhaps in all the various charms of English rural scenery is more attractive than the shady lane bordered by aged elms that leads to the ancient village church, embowered amidst its quiet trees, yet soon the traveller will enjoy their sight no more, and no longer will young lovers say :—

"How sweet the moonlight sleeps upon this bank."

But in many places the Church Walk goes not only up to the church, but by it, affording a right of way through the churchyard, and in this way bringing home to many thoughtful minds the quaint and curious lessons engraved on the old tombstones that border the path. But in one parish in the South of England, that I know, the Walk goes right through the Church, thus enabling parishioners to walk through their parish church at all times of the day (I think the doors are closed at sunset) and probably many have been glad to rest there in quiet for a few moments and think, and let us hope sometimes pray!

Strangely enough antiquaries seem never to have paid much attention to these old "Church Walks," yet they are a distinct feature of our church and its history. Many an old rate book would probably give items of interest concerning them, as showing how they were maintained and at what expense; but they are fast being transformed into roads or thoroughfares, and unless the devastating hand is stayed, one of the prettiest features of English rural life will soon be only a reminiscence.

Westminster Wax-Works.

By William Andrews.

AT the commencement of the Queen's reign, one of the sights of London was the wax-works at Westminster Abbey. In 1834, however, Madame Tussaud had established her famous exhibition, and the show at Westminster waned; with diminished receipts it was discontinued in 1839, after it had been for ages a source of considerable profit to the Abbey officials. For many years the effigies had been closed to the general public, and lost sight of; popular guides did not refer to them, and only by special order of the Dean could they be inspected. Dean Bradley, appreciating the antiquarian value of the figures, has thrown them open to sightseers once more, on payment of a small sum of money for admission to the Islip Chapel, where they are kept in glass cases.

In Saxon and Norman times, it was the practise when a monarch passed away to embalm the body, then dress it in costly regal robes, with a crown on the head, and with much pomp carry it on a bier to its final resting-place.

From ancient chronicles may be gleaned interesting particulars of the stately funerals of mediæval times. Henry II. died in 1189, and his obsequies are described by an old chronicler. "He was cloathed," it is recorded, "in Royal Robes, his Crown upon his Head, white gloves upon his

FUNERAL OF RICHARD II. *(From an early MS. of Froissart).*

Hands, Boots of Gold upon his Legs, gilt Spurs upon his Heels, a great ring upon his Finger, his Sceptre in his Hande, his Sworde by his side, and his Face uncovered and all bare." Such is the brief but informing account of a royal funeral.

Prior to the interment of the body, it lay in state for a considerable time, and on either side of it lighted tapers were placed, and attendants stood wearing hoods drawn over their heads. In the Middle Ages, burials were much longer deferred than they are in these later times. We may point out in proof of this statement, that the Black Prince died on June 8th, 1376, and that he was not interred until after Michaelmas of the same year. His widow died on August 7th, 1385, and it was not until the 7th of December following that letters were issued to the peers to attend her funeral.

With the English era which followed the Norman rule, a change in the manner of conducting royal funerals was introduced. Lead coffins enclosed the body, and instead of exposing the corpse, a carved figure of wood, as natural in appearance as art could make it, dressed in the robes of the departed, was carried in the funeral procession, and deposited in the Abbey. In some instances, leather, plaster of Paris, and other materials were employed in making the effigies. Later, in the time of Elizabeth, and possibly a century earlier, the figures were modelled of wax, casts of the faces were taken, and with the aid of wigs, etc., almost life-like representations were made.

A herse, or hearse, it is spelled both ways in old-time records, was used at funerals. We must not confuse it with the modern hearse. It was a temple-shaped structure of wood, richly-decorated

HERSE OF JAMES I. *(Designed by Inigo Jones).*

with banners, hatchments bearing the arms of the deceased, draped and gilded, and no pains and expense were spared in beautifying it. A leading architect would design it. Inigo Jones planned the one for James I., and it is stated that he made the draperies of the statues that adorned it of white calico and starch, and the heads of plaster of Paris. This king's funeral was conducted with much ceremony. Provision was made for placing lighted candles on the herse. When a funeral arrived at the Abbey, the wax effigy was deposited under the herse, and the coffin lowered into the grave. The herse remained for some time in the Abbey, depending greatly on the rank of the person to whose memory it was placed, or the requirements for space made by the death of others. Chaucer, in his " Dream," refers to the practice of offering up prayers round the herse.

> " And after that about the herse
> Many oresons and verses
> Without note full softly
> Said were, and that full heartily,
> That all the night, till it was day,
> The people in the church can pray,
> Unto the Holy Trinity,
> On those soules to have pity."

It was customary to pin short poems or epitaphs of a laudatory character on the herses. The best example that has come down to us is the epitaph by Ben Jonson on the Countess of Pembroke :—

> " Underneath this sable herse
> Lies the subject of all verse,
> Sidney's sister, Pembroke's mother.
> Death! ere thou hast slain another,
> Fair, and wise, and good as she,
> Time shall throw a dart at thee."

We read that on Bloody Mary's herse were set up angels of wax, and the valence was fringed and adorned with escutcheons.

Mary, the queen of William III., died in 1694, and the last herse used in this country was the one under which her effigy was placed in Westminster Abbey. An interesting circumstance connected with her funeral may be mentioned: it was the first ever attended by both Houses of Parliament in state. The Lords appeared in their robes of scarlet and ermine, and the Commons in long black mantles.

Drawings of herses made of wood are by no means rare, but not a single example of a herse of wood has come down to us, as far as we are able to discover. Some herses constructed of iron have survived the changes of three centuries. We give an illustration from the pencil of Mr. Thomas R. Macquoid of a good example over the tomb of Robert Marmion and his wife, in Tanfield Church, near Ripon. It will be observed

WESTMINSTER WAX-WORKS. 281

that it has sconces for holding seven candles.

There are only a few funeral effigies extant, but in the pages of history may be found many

HERSE AT THE MARMION TOMB, TANSFIELD.

allusions to them. They can be traced back in Westminster Abbey to the fourteenth century. The earliest example of which we have been able to find any account is that of Edward the First. Dryden, writing in 1658, names, in addition to Edward I., the figures of Henry V., Henry VII., James I., and their queens, also Prince Henry and Queen Elizabeth. The effigies of Edward III., and Phillipa, noticed by Stow in the preceding century, appear to have disappeared before Dryden's day. It was customary to remove effigies when they were old and shabby, and when the space they filled was wanted for others. Dart, in his "Westmonasterium," has some notes on the royal effigies. "There are many of them," says Dart, "sadly mangled, some with their faces broke, others broken in sunder, and most of them stripped of their robes, I suppose by the late rebels. I observe the ancientest have escaped best, I suppose by reason their cloaths were too old for booty. There is, I take it, Edward III. with a large robe, once of crimson velvet, but now appears like leather. There is Henry V., but I can't suppose it is that carried at his funeral, for it was made of tann'd leather, but this is of wood, as are all the old ones. The later are of stuff, having the heads only of wood, as Queen Elizabeth, who is entirely stripped, and James I."

Walpole was familiar with the figures, and

frequently visited the Abbey with his friends to see them. "You will smile," he wrote in one of his letters, "when I tell you that t'other day a party went to Westminster Abbey, and among the rest saw the ragged regiment. They enquired the names of the figures, 'I don't know them,' said the man, 'but if Mr. Walpole were here he could tell you every one.'" The old and broken effigies are not exhibited, a few only of the more modern examples are on view.

The weird effigy of Queen Elizabeth attracts the chief attention. Here she is represented as she appeared in old age, but this is not the figure carried at her funeral. She died in 1603, and by 1708 the original effigy was worn out, and we learn from a chronicler of the period, that the only remains of her royal robes, which in the past has attracted so much admiration, was "a dirty old ruff." The figure was restored by the Chapter in 1760, and the face is said to be a copy of that on her tomb. It is a small face, wrinkled about the chin and neck, but the features are delicate, the eyes expressive and bright. She appears arrogant, and an ill-tempered expression on the face renders it far from pleasing. The costume is interesting, and is an exact imitation of a part of the Queen's extensive wardrobe. The bodice is of ruby velvet heavily embroidered with silver, long-waisted and pointed. It is low at the shoulders, displaying a scraggy neck. To accentuate the slimness of the tightly compressed waist, the hips are padded about a foot out on both sides. The petticoat is of the same colour and material as the bodice, but the over-skirt, cut away from the front, is of dark brown velvet. The petticoat is short, leaving exposed to view a neat ankle and small arched though broad foot in a dainty shoe with enormous bows. Elizabeth was vain of her feet, and had all dresses short in front to display them.

Charles II.'s effigy is the oldest of the original figures, now in a sufficient state of preservation to be on view, and is said to be a contemporary portrait modelled at the time of his death. It stood for two centuries above his grave in the south aisle of Henry VII.'s chapel, and was his only monument. When the king came to the throne the nation was full of rejoicing, pomp and magnificence prevailed, the people were mad with joy, and chroniclers confessed that they could not do justice when describing the glories of the festivities. This contrasts strangely with his funeral, for we are told by Evelyn, that "he was

EFFIGY OF CHARLES II.

obscurely buried at night without any manner of pomp, and soon forgotten after all his vanity." The "Merry Monarch" was a personable personage, and the wax figure represents him as a handsome man. His eyes are dark and mournful, and dark hair is flowing over his shoulders. The robes he wears are those of the order of the garter, and are of blue and red velvet, the ermine which edges them is of the dirtiest and dustiest description, and the beautiful and real point lace at his neck and wrists is perfectly brown with age. It must be conceded that the face is ghastly as are all the others, but it is a fine example of the art of modelling in wax, and gives a good idea of the true appearance of this pleasure-loving monarch.

Very interesting are the effigies of William and Mary, which are both in one case. William is a slight short man, whilst Mary is tall and imposing, and so the king is elevated on a footstool, but even then is not up to his wife in stature. His face is expressive, the eyes are hawk-like, the thin lips, the broad brow all bespeak the master soul within; his whole appearance seems to indicate the conquest of spirit over nature, for his frame is puny in the extreme. Mary is imposing yet not striking in feature or figure. She wears a fine brocaded shirt, and a purple dress over it, and is laden with paste and imitation pearls, black with age.

Close by is Queen Anne sitting in a chair. Her figure is heavy and gigantic, and utterly devoid of grace. The face is full and pale, the eyes small and dark, and her dark hair hangs loose over her shoulders. Her dress is of rich yellow satin heavily embroidered, a state mantle falls round her, fastened on the shoulders by strings of large discoloured imitation pearls. A resplendent crown is on her head, in her hands are the sceptre and the orb, and round her neck the order of St. George. The face is from a cast taken after death.

Catherine, Duchess of Buckinghamshire, and her little son, the Marquis of Normanby, stand in a case together. The Duchess is dressed in the costume she wore at the coronation of George II. The petticoat is a wondrously embroidered brocade of purple and yellow, and the skirt is of rich velvet sweeping far behind. In such a bad light is the effigy placed that the costly robes look dingier even than the others.

In the centre of the chapel lies the effigy of the

EFFIGY OF SHEFFIELD, DUKE OF BUCKINGHAMSHIRE.

Duchess's last surviving son, Edmund Sheffield, the last Duke of Buckinghamshire. At the early age of nineteen he died at Rome, and was brought to England for interment. The bereaved mother tried to induce the Duchess of Marlborough to allow the body to be taken to the abbey on the car that had been used for the great Duke of Marlborough, but the request was haughtily refused. The Duchess of Buckinghamshire boasted that an undertaker had promised to supply a much finer car for £20. This effigy, which is magnificiently dressed, was the last ever carried at a funeral. A velvet cloak edged with ermine is thrown back, and displays a coat fastened down in front, and reaching to the knees, which is of most beautiful and costly texture. The ground is a delicate pink silk, but little of this is visible, so thickly is it embroidered with every imaginable shade of blending colours. This figure is laid at full length as though laid in state, and has a very impressive effect.

Frances, Duchess of Richmond, widow of the last of this noble line, the "La Belle Stuart" of Charles II.'s court, stands in the robes she wore at the coronation of Queen Anne. It is stated that she was the model for the figure of Britannia on our coins, and judging from the effigy there is no reason to doubt the statement. The imperial pose of the small stately head is exactly the same as that with which we are all familiar. Her dress of richly embroidered brocade, and trimmed with exquisite lace is excessively beautiful. By her side is perched a parrot, said to be in memory of one which the Duchess possessed for over forty years, and which only survived her a few days.

The foregoing are all the effigies that are connected with the custom under consideration. The number of sightseers decreased when no fresh attractions were introduced in the form of new effigies, and something had to be done to increase the scanty incomes of the minor canons and lay vicars. The first figure set up was that of the great Pitt, the Earl of Chatham. A guide book published in 1783, after describing the funeral effigies, states, " what eclipses the brilliancy of those effigies is the figure of the great Earl of Chatham in his parliamentry robes, lately (1779) introduced at considerable expense. It so well represents the original that there is nothing wanting but real life, for it seems to speak as you approach it." The pose is grand and dignified, in his hand is a folded document, and round his neck is the order of St. George. It is a beautifully finished figure in every respect. When Chatham's effigy was introduced the fee for seeing the waxworks was advanced from 3d. to 6d.

The last figure we have to notice is that of Lord Nelson, said to be modelled from a smaller one for which he sat. It is of considerable interest for the figure is attired in the clothes he wore with the exception of the coat. His waistcoat and breeches are of a white material, and his stockings are also white. The compilers of "The Deanery Guide to Westminster Abbey," quoting from *Notes and Queries*, of Nov. 17, 1883, say: "There is convincing proof that the hat belonged to the Admiral, for when Maclise painted 'The Death of Nelson' he borrowed it to copy, and found the eye patch still attached to the inner lining, and the stamp, always found in old hats of that period, in the crown. The makers were obliged to put it in to show that the 'hat tax' had been paid. Nelson was blind in his left eye. He is without his right arm which he lost in battle. On the left shoulder is a brass pin or nail, showing where the fatal bullet struck him. At his side hangs his sword, and numerous medals are on his breast." In 1805 Nelson was buried at St. Paul's, and his grave was the chief attraction of London, crowds going to see it. The Abbey of Westminster was deserted, but when the Admiral's effigy

GENERAL MONK. *(From "A Guide to the Wax-works at Westminster Abbey," 1768).*

was set up, the novelty-loving people returned. After the death of Cromwell, General Monk, Duke of Albemarle, had much to do with bringing

Charles II. to the throne. His figure, clad in full armour, used to stand next to that of the king, but the battered remains now find a place in a corner. On his head used to be a cap which is now missing, and which the guide used to hand round; it is referred to in "The Ingoldsby Legends":—

> I thought on Naseby—Marston Moor—on Worcester's 'crowning fight;'
> When on mine ear a sound there fell—it chilled me with affright,
> As thus in low, unearthly tones, I heard a voice begin,
> —'This here's the Cap of Giniral Monk!—Sir!—please put summut in!'

Index.

Adel, knocker at, 181
Aethelingey, 7
Alborough, Holderness, early carving at, 194
Alfred's Abbey Church, 7
All Saints' Church, York, knocker at, 182
Amiens, Cathedral of, 148
Ampulla, 135
Anchorage, 82-83
Anchorite, 80
Andrews, William, Fortified Church Towers, 105-111 Westminster Wax-Works, 275-295
Animals of the Church, in Wood, Stone, and Bronze, 168-200
Animals sacrificed, 33
Anne, Queen, Effigy of, 288
Arimathæa, St. Joseph of, 6
Art in the Primitive church, 206-207
Ashby-de-la-Zouch, Hermit of, 94-95
Athelstan, King, 27

Badges worn by Pilgrims, 155
Bagpipes, 186
Baiting Animals, 103
Banner of Templars, 114
Barker, Rev. J. Hudson, Hermits and Hermit cells, 68-96
Barton-on-Humber, St. Peter's Church at, 10
Beaver, 187
Bedale Church, 108
Bigg, John, Hermit, 93
Black Prince, Funeral of the, 277
Blackmore Church, 16-19
Blood of St. Thomas, 135
Blyth Church, Doom at, 221
Books on Knight-Templars, 124, 125
Bolton, Cumberland, Font at, 231

Bosava, ghost-laying at, 254-257
Botathen, ghost-laying at, 241-249
Bradford during the Civil War, 111
Brenge, frescoes at, 25
Britannia, Model for, 291-292
Buckinghamshire, Duchess of, 288
Burgh-on-the-Sand, 106
Buryan Church, 27

Caley, Rev. W. B. Russell; Church Walks, 269-274
Camel, 189
Candlemas Day, 233
Candles in the Church, 227
Canon authorising exorcism, 241
Canterbury Tales, 134, 155
Canute, 129
Castle Hedington; skin on church door, 159
Cat, 183-184, 185
Cat and fiddle, 183-184, 187, 188
Catfield, frescoes at, 214
Caxton, 142
Chadkirk, 15, 16
Chatham, Earl of, effigy of, 292
Charles II., effigy of, 284-287
Chester-le-Street, hermitage at, 85
Christmas, Flowers at, 230-231, 238
Church Wakes, 97-104
Church Walks, 269-274
Churchyards, fairs and markets not to be held in, 98-99
Cock, 197
Cock-fighting, 103
Conquest of Cornwall, memorial church, 27
Cornwall, Curious Churches of, 21-28; Wells of, 36-43; ghost-laying in, 241-261, 263-268
Costume of Templars, 113

Copford, skin on church door, 159, 163
Crocodile, 189
Cross Canonby, Roman font at, 239
Crow, 198
Crowland Abbey, 7, 84
Crusades, 112, 146
Crowle, mural painting discovered at, 214
Crypt at Canterbury Cathedral, quaint picture in, 213-214
Curious Churches in Cornwall, 21-28
Cursing Wells, 58
Cuthbert, St., legend of, 6
Cyrene, 2

Dalston, Holy Well near, 57
Dancing prohibited in churches, 99
Danes, 12, 158-167
Darkness devouring light, 174, 175
Deans of Middleham, 108-109
Death of a language, 28
Dedication day, flowers at, 231-232
Deer, 188
De Molay burnt to death, 119
Denton, hermit of, 93-94
Devil lore, 60
Dissolution of monasteries, 228
Dodge, Rev. Richard, ghost layer, 252-254
Dog, 184
Doom-well, 42
Dooms, 214-221
Dove, 199
Dragons, 176, 177, 178, 179, 180
Dragon killers, 176, 177, 178
Droitwich, customs at, 56
Druids, 187
Drum-like sounds from a well, 47
Durham Cathedral, frescoes at, 214; knocker at, 182, 184
Durham, stave church at, 10

Eagle, 194-195
Earl's Barton, 9
Easby, paintings at, 221
Easter, flowers at, 231, 236, 240
Ebbing and flowing well, 48-49
Edward I., death of, 106
Edwin, King, baptised, 6

Edmund, St., 11-13
Elephant, 188
Elizabeth, effigy of, 283
English Mediæval Pilgrimages, 129-144
Egypt, pilgrimages to, 145
Epitaphs on hearses, 279-280
Epworth, ghost at, 261-262
Erasmus, 155
Eskdale, hermitage at, 85

Fairs and markets forbidden to be held in churchyards, 98-99
Favourite saints, 35
Fen districts, hermits in, 83
Fire-places in church towers, 107, 108
Fish, 60-61, 199-200, 184
Flavel, Rev. Thomas, ghost layer, 249-252
Flowers and the Rites of the Church, 227-240
Floods, 176
Food of Templars, 113
Fordham, Bishop of Durham, 153
Fortified church-towers, 105-111
Fox, 192-193
Frescoes, 25, 27
Friend, Rev. H., Flowers and the rites of the church, 227-240
Funeral effigies, 275-295
Funeral of a hermit, 95-96
Funerals deferred, 277

Garland-wells, 52
Glastonbury, 6; well at, 61
Gloucester Cathedral, doom at, 220
Ghost-Layers and Ghost-Laying, 241-268
Goat's head, 173
Godefroi de St. Omer, 112
Great Salkeld, 105-106
Greenstead Church, 11-14
Groom, Demon, 261
Guides for Pilgrims, 142-143
Gunwallo Church, 27

Hadstock, skin on church door, 159
Hagioscopes, 83
Hagoday, 181-183
Haltwhistle, gravestone at, 132

INDEX.

Hambledon hermitage, 81
Hart, 188
Haslewood, Rev. Francis; Queries in Stone, 201-204
Hawk, 189, 198
Hawker, Rev. R. S., on ghost-laying, 242
Heathen lands, ceremonial use of flowers in, 227
Hermits and Hermit-Cells, 68-96
Hen and chickens, 198
Henry II., Funeral of, 276
Heron, 198
Herse, 278-281; last used, 280
Hexham Abbey, 85
Hetterdal Church, 3, 5
Holly, 230
Holme-Cultram, 106-107
Holy Land, Pilgrimages to the, 129
Holy Rood, 236
Holy Sepulchre in Jerusalem Church of, 120
Holy Thursday, dressing wells on, 54
Holy Trinity Church, Hull, 178
Holy Wells, 29-67
Hooper, on pictures in churches, 212-213
Hospitallers, 121
Human sacrifices, 33
Human Skin on Church Doors, 158-167
Hugo de Payens, 112
Hunting scenes, 189
Hyena, 189

Ichneumon, 189
Insanity, wells for curing, 35
Ireland, holy wells in, 60-61

Jago, Rev. M., ghost-layer, 260-261
James I., hearse of, 278-279
Jerusalem, pilgrimages to, 145
Jones, Inigo, design of herse by, 278

Kelso monastery, 74
Knaresborough, hermitage at, 93, 94, 95
Knights Templars: their churches and their privileges, 112-128
Knockers, 181-183

Lach-Szyma, Rev. W. S., Curious Churches in Cornwall, 21-28
Lamb, badge of Templars, 114
Landewednack, 27
Lanreath, ghosts at, 253
Lawful sports, 102
Lead coffins, 277
Lindisfarne, 7
Lion, 180-183
Lioness bringing forth her young dead, 181
Legend of the first Christian Church, 6
Lords of misrule not to enter the church, 100
Lotus and religious rites, 227
Lourdes, pilgrimages to, 146
Lower Peover Church, 14
Lytchgates, 19
Lutterworth, fresco at, 209; doom at, 215

Malmsbury Abbey, 8
Maltese cross, 114
Manchester, Plays at, 103
Margaretting church, 19
Marmion, herse of, 280-281
Marton Church, 14-15
Mayence, lion knocker at, 182-183, 185
Mecca, pilgrimages to, 145
Melsonby church, 109
Menacuddle Well, 41
Middle Ages, funerals in the, 277
Middleham church, 108-109
Mineral springs, 61-62
Mistletoe, 238-239
Monk, General, 294-295
Monkey, 183, 185, 186
Morris-dancers, 100, 103
Mosaic in St. Paul's Cathedral, 222
Mullion, brass at, 250

Nelson, Lord, effigy of, 293-294
Newcastle-on-Tyne, steeple, 109; defence of the town, 110, Scotch prisoners placed about the steeple, 110
Newland, Worcestershire, 19
Newtown, Montgomeryshire, 19
Norfolk, stave churches in, 10
Norman funerals, 275

INDEX.

Normanby, Marquis of, effigy of, 288
Norway, wooden churches in, 3-5

Old Hermit of Newton Burgoland, 94-95
Orissa, Pilgrimages to, 145
Otter, 189
Owl, 198

Pagan customs, 30
Palm Sunday, 233, 238
Parish Feast, 101-102
Partridge, 198
Paul Church burnt by Spaniards, 27
Paul of the Thebaid, 75
Paulinus, St., preaching, 6
Pelican, 195-197
Pentreath, Dolly, 28
Penzance, Ghost at, 266-267
Pictures in Churches, 205-226
Pig, 186, 187, 190
Pilgrim in hair shirt and cloak, 132
Pilgrims' Signs, 145-157
Pillar saints, 77-78
Pin-Wells, 49-54
Poor soldiers of Christ, 113
Pope Alexander III. confirms privileges of Templars, 125
Privileges of Knights Templars, 125-128
Privileges of Pilgrims, 154
Puritans, 205-206
Purity, water symbol of, 32

Queries in Stones, 201-204

Rag-Wells, 52
Rams, 191
Raven, 199
Red Cross Knights, 120-121
Rees, J. Rogers, the Knight Templars: their churches and their privileges, 112-128
Rees, Rev. R. Wilkins; Ghost-Layers and Ghost-Laying, 241-268
Ribbesford Church, 19
Richard II., Funeral of, 276
Richmond, Duchess of, effigy of, 291-292
Robin Hood, pageant of, 103

Rochester, skin on Cathedral door, 160
Roman Britain, 4-5
Rome, pilgrimages to, 129; shrines in, 146
Round churches, 121
Rudall, Rev. W., on ghost-laying, 241-249
Rushbearing, 100
Russia, wooden churches in, 3, 4

Sabrina, legend of, 29
Sacrifices, human, 33
Sanctuary, 127
Sanctus Bell, 164
Saxon funerals, 275
Scallop shell, 133
Sea-dragon, 180
Sennen Church, 27
Serpent, 189
Settle, well at, 48-49
Sheffield, Duke of Buckinghamshire, effigy of, 288 291
Sheep, 191
Smarden Church, grotesque figure at, 201-204
Snail, 194
Spain, shrines in, 130-146
Spalding, stave church at, 10
South Leigh, doom at, 220
Squirrel, 190
St. Agatha, 190
St. Anthony, 187
St. Augustine of Hippo, 208
St. Austell, 25
St. Barnaby's Day, 235
St. Botolph, 84
St. Cuthbert, 56, 59, 86-87, 88, 130
St. Edmund, Pilgrims' signs of, 151
St. Elian, 58
St. George and the Dragon, 178
St. George, legend of, 23-24
St. George's well, 33
St. Germo, 26
St. Gregory's Church, Norwich, knocker at, 182, 183
St. Godric, 85-86
St. Guthlac, 83
St. Helen, 49
St. Hubert, 87, 188
St. Hugh at Lincoln, 130
St. James of Compostella, 141, 146

INDEX.

St. John the Baptist Day, 234, 238
St. John at Beverley, 130-138
St. John's Lee, Hexham, 85
St. Justinia, 190
St. Keyne, well of, 37, 39
St. Leonard, 153
St. Martin at Tours, 73, 146
St. Neot, 22
St. Oswald's well, legend of, 58
St. Paulinus, 208
St. Peter, 197
St. Robert of Knaresborough, 93
St. Swithin, ghost at, 263-266
St. Swithin at Winchester, 130
St. Thomas à Becket, 130, 146, 147; Pilgrims' signs of, 149-151
St. Tecla's well, 47-48
St. William at York, 130
St. Winifred's well, 43-47
Stratford-on-Avon, doom at, 214-215
Stalls forbidden to be set within the church, 98
Stations of the Cross, 223-224
Stave-Kirks, 1-20
Stock Church, 19
Stocks, Parish, 271-272
Sun-worship, 173, 175
Swans, 174
Symbolism of animals, 168-200
Syra, pilgrimages to, 145

Talland Church, devil-lore relating to, 252
Tansfield, hearse at, 280-281
Templars' churches and houses, 120-125
Temple Church, 120, 122-124
Temples of the East, 227-228
Thompson, W. H., English Mediæval Pilgrimages, 129-144
Thor's well, 33
Tissington, well-dressing at, 54
Turtle dove, 198
Tutelary deities, 33
Tyack, Rev. G. S.: Stave-Kirks, 1-20; Pilgrims' Signs, 145-157; Human Skins on Church Doors, 158-167; Pictures in Churches, 205-221
Typhon, 175, 177

Ulk, 194

Unicorn, 190, 191, 192
Urnes Church, 3

Virgin Mary, 190

Wakes, Church, 97-104; origin of name, 97
Walks, Church, 269-274
Walpole and Wax-works, 282-283
Walpole St. Andrews, 82
Walters, Cuming: Holy Wells, 29-67
Walter de Bolebec, 74
Walsingham, Our Lady of, 130, 136, 152
Warkworth Hermitage, 72, 88-93
Water-kelpie, 30
Wavertree well, 60
Wealth of the Templars, 115-119
Welford Wake, 99
Wells dedicated to Christian saints, 31-32; Well-worship, 34, 64-67; Dressing, 54-57; Visited at sunrise in May, 55
Wenhaston Doom, 215-219
Wesley, Rev. John, 261
Westminster Abbey, skin on door, 160, 161, 163-165; Monks thrown into the Tower, 165-166; Wax-works, 275-295
Whale, 191-192
Whitsuntide Ales, 202; Flowers at, 232
Whitewashing pictures, 213
Wildridge, T. Tindall; Animals of the Church in Wood, Stone, and Bronze, 168-200
William and Mary, effigy of, 287-288
Windows of St. Neot, 23
Withes, churches constructed of, 2-3
Woden's well, 33
Wolf, 189
Wood, use of in architecture, 1
Wooden churches, 1-20
Woods, Rev. Mr., ghost layer, 258-260
Womersley Church, curious picture at, 223
Wool-packs used for protecting a church, 111
Worchester, skin on Cathedral door, 160, 161-162, 164
Wyverns, 174

"Mr. Andrews' books are always interesting."—*Church Bells*

"No student of Mr. Andrews' books can be a dull after-dinner speaker, for his writings are full of curious out-of-the-way information and good stories."—*Birmingham Daily Gazette*.

England in the Days of Old.

BY WILLIAM ANDREWS, F.R.H.S.,

Demy 8vo., 7s. 6d.   Numerous Illustrations.

THIS volume is one of unusual interest and value to the lover of olden days and ways, and can hardly fail to interest and instruct the reader. It recalls many forgotten episodes, scenes, characters, manners, customs, etc., in the social and domestic life of England.

CONTENTS :—When Wigs were Worn—Powdering the Hair—Men Wearing Muffs—Concerning Corporation Customs—Bribes for the Palate—Rebel Heads on City Gates—Burial at Cross Roads—Detaining the Dead for Debt—A Nobleman's Household in Tudor Times—Bread and Baking in Bygone Days—Arise, Mistress, Arise!—The Turnspit—A Gossip about the Goose—Bells as Time-Tellers—The Age of Snuffing—State Lotteries—Bear-Baiting—Morris Dancers—The Folk-Lore of Midsummer Eve—Harvest Home—Curious Charities—An Old-Time Chronicler.

LIST OF ILLUSTRATIONS :—The House of Commons in the time of Sir Robert Walpole—Egyptian Wig—The Earl of Albemarle—Campaign Wig—Periwig with Tail—Ramillie-Wig—Pig-tail Wig—Bag-Wig—Archbishop Tilotson—Heart-Breakers—A Barber's Shop in the time of Queen Elizabeth—With and Without a Wig—Stealing a Wig—Man with Muff, 1693—Burying the Mace at Nottingham—The Lord Mayor of York escorting Princess Margaret—The Mayor of Wycombe going to the Guildhall—Woman wearing a Scold's Bridle—The Brank—Andrew Marvell—Old London Bridge, shewing heads of rebels on the gate—Axe, Block, and Executioner's Mask—Margaret Roper taking leave of her father, Sir Thomas More—Rebel Heads, from a print published in 1746—Temple Bar in Dr. Johnson's time—Micklegate Bar, York—Clock, Hampton Court Palace—Drawing a Lottery in the Guildhall, 1751—Advertising the Last State Lottery—Partaking of the Pungent Pinch—Morris Dance, from a painted window at Betley—Morris Dance, temp. James I.—A Whitsun Morris Dance—Bear Garden, or Hope Theatre, 1647—The Globe Theatre, temp. Elizabeth—Plan of Bankside early in the Seventeenth Century—John Stow's Monument.

A carefully prepared Index enables the reader to refer to the varied and interesting contents of the book.

"A very attractive and informing book."—*Birmingham Daily Gazette*.

"Mr. Andrews has the true art of narration, and contrives to give us the results of his learning with considerable freshness of style, whilst his subjects are always interesting and picturesque."—*Manchester Courier*.

"The book is of unusual interest."—*Eastern Morning News*.

"Of the many clever books which Mr. Andrews has written none does him greater credit than "England in the Days of Old," and none will be read with greater profit."—*Northern Gazette*.

Antiquities and Curiosities of the Church.

Edited by WILLIAM ANDREWS, f.r.h.s.

Demy 8vo., 7s. 6d.   Numerous Illustrations.

Contents :—Church History and Historians—Supernatural Interference in Church Building—Ecclesiastical Symbolism in Architecture—Acoustic Jars—Crypts—Heathen Customs at Christian Feasts—Fish and Fasting—Shrove-tide and Lenten Customs—Wearing Hats in Church—The Stool of Repentance—Cursing by Bell, Book, and Candle—Pulpits—Church Windows—Alms-Boxes and Alms-Dishes—Old Collecting Boxes—Gargoyles—Curious Vanes—People and Steeple Rhymes—Sun-Dials—Jack of the Clock-House—Games in Churchyards—Circular Churchyards—Church and Churchyard Charms and Cures—Yew Trees in Churchyards.

"A very entertaining work."—*Leeds Mercury.*

"A well-printed, handsome, and profusely illustrated work."—*Norfolk Chronicle.*

"There is much curious and interesting reading in this popular volume, which moreover has a useful index."—*Glasgow Herald.*

"The contents of the volume is exceptionally good reading, and crowded with out-of-the way, useful, and well selected information on a subject which has an undying interest."—*Birmingham Mercury.*

"In concluding this notice it is only the merest justice to add that every page of it abounds with rare and often amusing information, drawn from the most accredited sources. It also abounds with illustrations of our old English authors, and it is likely to prove welcome not only to the Churchman, but to the student of folk-lore and of poetical literature."—*Morning Post.*

"We can recommend this volume to all who are interested in the notable and curious things that relate to churches and public worship in this and other countries."—*Newcastle Daily Journal.*

"It is very handsomely got up and admirably printed, the letterpress being beautifully clear."—*Lincoln Mercury.*

"The book is well indexed."—*Daily Chronicle.*

"By delegating certain topics to those most capable of treating them, the editor has the satisfaction of presenting the best available information in a very attractive manner."—*Dundee Advertiser.*

"It must not be supposed that the book is of interest only to Churchmen, although primarily so, for it treats in such a skilful and instructive manner with ancient manners and customs as to make it an invaluable book of reference to all who are concerned in the seductive study of antiquarian subjects."—*Chester Courant.*

The Miracle Play in England,

An Account of the Early Religious Drama.

By SIDNEY W. CLARKE, Barrister-at-Law.

Crown 8vo., 3s. 6d. Illustrated.

In bygone times the Miracle Play formed an important feature in the religious life of England. To those taking an interest in the history of the Church of England, this volume will prove useful. The author has given long and careful study to this subject, and produced a reliable and readable book, which can hardly fail to interest and instruct the reader. It is a volume for general reading, and for a permanent place in the reference library.

Contents :—The Origin of Drama—The Beginnings of English Drama—The York Plays—The Wakefield Plays—The Chester Plays—The Coventry Plays—Other English Miracle Plays—The Production of a Miracle Play—The Scenery, Properties, and Dresses—Appendix—The Order of the York Plays—Extract from City Register of York, 1426—The Order of the Wakefield Plays—The Order of the Chester Plays—The Order of the Grey Friars' Plays at Coventry—A Miracle Play in a Puppet Show—Index.

"Mr. Clarke has chosen a most interesting subject, one that is attractive alike to the student, the historian, and the general reader . . . . A most interesting volume, and a number of quaint illustrations add to its value."—*Birmingham Daily Gazette.*

"The book should be useful to many."—*Manchester Guardian.*

"An admirable work."—*Eastern Morning News.*

"Mr. Sidney Clarke's concise monograph in 'The Miracle Play in England' is another of the long and interesting series of antiquarian volumes for popular reading issued by the same publishing house. The author briefly sketches the rise and growth of the 'Miracle' or 'Mystery' play in Europe and in England; and gives an account of the series or cycle of these curious religious dramas—the forerunners of the modern secular play—performed at York, Wakefield, Chester, Coventry, and other towns in the middle ages. But his chief efforts are devoted to giving a sketch of the manner of production, and the scenery, properties, and dresses of the old miracle play, as drawn from the minute account books of the craft and trade guilds and other authentic records of the period. Mr. Clarke has gone to the best sources for his information, and the volume, illustrated by quaint cuts, is an excellent compendium of information on a curious byeway of literature and art."—*The Scotsman.*

Historic Dress of the Clergy.

BY THE REV. GEO. S. TYACK, B.A.,

Author of "The Cross in Ritual, Architecture, and Art."

Crown, cloth extra, 3s. 6d.

The work contains thirty-three illustrations from ancient monuments, rare manuscripts, and other sources.

"A very painstaking and very valuable volume on a subject which is just now attracting much attention. Mr. Tyack has collected a large amount of information from sources not available to the unlearned, and has put together his materials in an attractive way. The book deserves and is sure to meet with a wide circulation."—*Daily Chronicle.*

"This book is written with great care, and with an evident knowledge of history. It is well worth the study of all who wish to be better informed upon a subject which the author states in his preface gives evident signs of a lively and growing interest."—*Manchester Courier.*

"Those who are interested in the Dress of the Clergy will find full information gathered together here, and set forth in a lucid and scholarly way."—*Glasgow Herald.*

"We are glad to welcome yet another volume from the author of 'The Cross in Ritual, Architecture, and Art.' His subject, chosen widely and carried out comprehensively, makes this a valuable book of reference for all classes. It is only the antiquary and the ecclesiologist who can devote time and talents to research of this kind, and Mr. Tyack has done a real and lasting service to the Church of England by collecting so much useful and reliable information upon the dress of the clergy in all ages, and offering it to the public in such a popular form. We do not hesitate to recommend this volume as the most reliable and the most comprehensive illustrated guide to the history and origin of the canonical vestments and other dress worn by the clergy, whether ecclesiastical, academical, or general, while the excellent work in typography and binding make it a beautiful gift-book."—*Church Bells.*

"A very lucid history of ecclesiastical vestments from Levitical times to the present day."—*Pall Mall Gazette.*

"The book can be recommended to the undoubtedly large class of persons who are seeking information on this and kindred subjects."—*The Times.*

"The work may be read either as pastime or for instruction, and is worthy of a place in the permanent section of any library. The numerous illustrations, extensive contents table and index, and beautiful workmanship, both in typography and binding, are all features of attraction and utility."—*Dundee Advertiser.*

The Cross in Ritual, Architecture, and Art.

By the Rev. GEO. S. TYACK, b.a.

Crown 8vo., 3s. 6d. Numerous Illustrations.

The Author of this Volume has brought together much valuable and out-of-the-way information which cannot fail to interest and instruct the reader. The work is the result of careful study, and its merits entitle it to a permanent place in public and private libraries. Many beautiful illustrations add to the value of the Volume.

"This book is reverent, learned, and interesting, and will be read with a great deal of profit by anyone who wishes to study the history of the sign of our Redemption."—*Church Times.*

"A book of equal interest to artists, archæologists, architects, and the clergy has been written by the Rev. G. S. Tyack, upon 'The Cross in Ritual, Architecture, and Art.' Although Mr. Tyack has restricted himself to this country, this work is sufficiently complete for its purpose, which is to show the manifold uses to which the Cross, the symbol of the Christian Faith, has been put in Christian lands. It treats of the Cross in ritual, in Church ornament, as a memorial of the dead, and in secular mason work; of preaching crosses, wayside and boundary crosses, well crosses, market crosses, and the Cross in heraldry. Mr. Tyack has had the assistance of Mr. William Andrews, to whom he records his indebtedness for the use of his collection of works, notes, and pictures; but it is evident that this book has cost many years of research on his own part. It is copiously and well illustrated, lucidly ordered and written, and deserves to be widely known."—*Yorkshire Post.*

"This is an exhaustive treatise on a most interesting subject, and Mr. Tyack has proved himself to be richly informed and fully qualified to deal with it. All lovers of ecclesiastical lore will find the volume instructive and suggestive, while the ordinary reader will be surprised to find that the Cross in the churchyard or by the roadside has so many meanings and significances. Mr. Tyack divides his work into eight sections, beginning with the pre-Christian cross, and then tracing its development, its adaptations, its special uses, and applications, and at all times bringing out clearly its symbolic purposes. We have the history of the Cross in the Church, of its use as an ornament, and of its use as a public and secular instrument; then we get a chapter on 'Memorial Crosses,' and another on 'Wayside and Boundary Cross.' The volume teems with facts, and it is evident that Mr. Tyack has made his study a labour of love, and spared no research in order, within the prescribed limits, to make his work complete. He has given us a valuable work of reference, and a very instructive and entertaining volume."—*Birmingham Daily Gazette.*

"An engrossing and instructive narrative."—*Dundee Advertiser.*

"As a popular account of the Cross in history, we do not know that a better book can be named."—*Glasgow Herald.*

Legal Lore: Curiosities of Law and Lawyers.

Edited by WILLIAM ANDREWS, F.R.H.S.

Demy 8vo., Cloth extra, 7s. 6d.

CONTENTS:—Bible Law—Sanctuaries—Trials in Superstitious Ages—On Symbols—Law Under the Feudal System—The Manor and Manor Law—Ancient Tenures—Laws of the Forest—Trial by Jury in Old Times—Barbarous Punishments—Trials of Animals—Devices of the Sixteenth Century Debtors—Laws Relating to the Gipsies—Commonwealth Law and Lawyers—Cock-Fighting in Scotland—Cockieleerie Law—Fatal Links—Post-Mortem Trials—Island Laws—The Little Inns of Court—Obiter.

"There are some very amusing and curious facts concerning law and lawyers. We have read with much interest the articles on Sanctuaries, Trials in Superstitious Ages, Ancient Tenures, Trials by Jury in Old Times, Barbarous Punishments, and Trials of Animals, and can heartily recommend the volume to those who wish for a few hours' profitable diversion in the study of what may be called the light literature of the law."—*Daily Mail.*

"Most amusing and instructive reading."—*The Scotsman.*

"The contents of the volume are extremely entertaining, and convey not a little information on ancient ideas and habits of life. While members of the legal profession will turn to the work for incidents with which to illustrate an argument or point a joke, laymen will enjoy its vivid descriptions of old-fashioned proceedings and often semi-barbaric ideas to obligation and rectitude."—*Dundee Advertiser.*

"The subjects chosen are extremely interesting, and contain a quantity of out-of-the-way and not easily accessible information. . . . Very tastefully printed and bound."—*Birmingham Daily Gazette.*

"The book is handsomely got up; the style throughout is popular and clear, and the variety of its contents, and the individuality of the writers gave an added charm to the work."—*Daily Free Press.*

"The book is interesting both to the general reader and the student."—*Cheshire Notes and Queries.*

"Those who care only to be amused will find plenty of entertainment in this volume, while those who regard it as a work of reference will rejoice at the variety of material, and appreciate the careful indexing."—*Dundee Courier.*

"Very interesting subjects, lucidly and charmingly written. The versatility of the work assures for it a wide popularity."—*Northern Gazette.*

"A happy and useful addition to current literature."—*Norfolk Chronicle.*

"The book is a very fascinating one, and it is specially interesting to students of history as showing the vast changes which, by gradual course of development have been brought about both in the principles and practice of the law."—*The Evening Gazette.*

Bygone Southwark.

BY MRS. E. BOGER.

Demy 8vo., Cloth gilt, 7s. 6d. Numerous Illustrations.

CONTENTS:—Historical Southwark and London Bridge—Ecclesiastical Southwark—Literary and Dramatic Southwark—Local and Antiquarian Southwark—The Industries of Southwark—Amusements of Southwark—Odds and Ends, Shreds and Patches—Index.

"An attractive volume."—*The Standard.*

"A popular and interesting volume. .... It will be prized by the local historian and antiquary, and will be read with delight by all interested in London annals. Its illustrations include views of St. Saviour's Church and reproductions of the Frost Fair, the Globe Theatre, the interior of the Swan Theatre by De Witt, the old Tabard Inn, old London Bridge, and other spots of high interest."—*Notes and Queries.*

Bygone Berkshire.

EDITED BY THE REV. P. H. DITCHFIELD, M.A., F.S.A.

Demy 8vo., Cloth gilt, 7s. 6d. Numerous Illustrations.

CONTENTS:—Historic Berkshire—Windsor Castle—Wallingford Castle—Cumnor Place and Amy Robsart—Alfred the Great—The Guilds of Berkshire—The Scouring of the White Horse—The Last of the Abbots—Siege of Reading—Reading Abbey—The First Battle of Newbury—The Second Battle of Newbury—Binfield and Easthampstead 1700-1716, and the Early Years of Alexander Pope—Berkshire Words and Phrases—Bull-Baiting in Berkshire—Index.

"'Bygone Berkshire' is a welcome addition to a series which we have often favourably noticed."—*The Times.*

"The volume is a handsome one, and its many illustrations have been carefully drawn."—*Reading Mercury.*

Bygone Somerset.

EDITED BY CUMING WALTERS.

Demy 8vo., Cloth gilt, 7s. 6d.

CONTENTS:—Somerset County—Sedgemoor and Monmouth Rebellion—Taunton and the Bloody Assize—Cliffs and Caverns—The Lead Mines of the Mendips—The Legends and Antiquities of Glastonbury—A Note on the Cathedral City of Wells—Church Bell Inscriptions—The Christian Symbol in Wood and Stone—The Camelot of History and Romance—Roman and Fashionable Bath—Clevedon: a Literary Shrine—Superstitions and Curious Events—Cider Songs and Customs—The Lansdown Bagdad and its Caliph—The Learned Friar of Ilchester—Queen Elizabeth's Godson—The Inland Sanctuaries—"Quorum Reliquæ Hic Sunt—The City and County of Bristol—Index.

"There is much that is readable and very enjoyable in its pages . . . The illustrations are excellent, and we can recommend this book to our readers with confidence."—*Bristol Times and Mirror.*

"Forms a most valuable addition to any library."—*Clevedon Mercury.*

Bygone Sussex.

By W. E. A. AXON.

Demy 8vo., Cloth gilt, 7s. 6d. Numerous Illustrations.

CONTENTS :—The Land of the South Saxons—Pardon Brasses—Trial of Henry Robson in 1598—In Denis Duval's Country—The Long Man of Wilmington—The True Maid of the South—' Old Humphrey's' Grave—A Mediæval Legend of Winchelsea—Poems of Sussex Places—Spirits at Brightling in 1659—The Monstrous Child of Chichester—A Ruskin Pilgramage—Rye in the Sixteenth and Seventeenth Centuries—The Merchant of Chichester—Drayton's Song of Sussex—A Sussex Book—The Mercer's Son of Midhurst—The Drummer of Herstmonceux—Sussex Sun-Dials—Tunbridge Wells Early in the Eighteenth Century—The Miller's Tomb—The Sussex Muse—Index.

" It is a most acceptable addition to Sussex literature."—*Brighton Herald.*

" A handsome volume."—*Manchester Guardian.*

" A very pleasant miscellany of topics relating to the Sussex of the past."—*The Times.*

Bygone Scotland.

By DAVID MAXWELL, C.E.

Demy 8vo., Cloth gilt, 7s. 6d. Numerous Illustrations.

CONTENTS :—The Roman Conquest of Britain—Britain as a Roman Province—The Anglo-Saxons in Britain—The Rise of the Scottish Nation—The Danish Invasions of Britain—The last Two Saxon Kings of England - How Scotland became a Free Nation—Scotland in the Two Hundred Years after Bannockburn—The Older Scottish Literature—The Reformation in England and Scotland—The Rival Queens, Mary and Elizabeth—Old Edinburgh—Offences and their Punishment in the Sixteenth Century—Old Aberdeen—Witchcraft in Scotland—Holy-Wells in Scotland—Scottish Marriage Customs—Scotland under Charles the First—Scot'and under Cromwell—Scotland under Charles the Second—Scotland under James the Second—The Revolution of 1688—The Massacre of Glencoe—The Union of Scotland and England—The Jacobite Risings of 1715—The Rebellion of 1745—Index.

" The book forms a splendid addition to the works of the same series all printed at the ' Hull Press,' and, like all its predecessors, is printed in the exceptionally beautiful style which marks the productions of Mr. Andrews' establishment. The volume is handsomely bound, and well illustrated. Mr. Andrews is a bookmaker *par excellence*."—*Printing World.*

" Scotland is decidedly a country ' with a past,' and that past Mr. Maxwell has here made real to us in a handsome volume, which is at once entertaining and instructive. All interested in the history of North Britain may be confidently recommended to add Mr. Maxwell's work to their shelves."—*Publishers' Circular.*

" A worthy addition to a series which has more than once been mentioned and commended in this place."—*The Times.*

Bygone Cheshire.

Edited by WILLIAM ANDREWS, F.R.H.S.

Demy 8vo., Cloth gilt, 7s. 6d. Numerous Illustrations.

Contents :—Historic Cheshire—King Edgar on the Dee—Chester Castle and Walls—Chester Cathedral—Festival Time in Old Chester—Chester Fair—The Origin of the Rows of Chester—Old Chester Houses—The Dee Mills and "The Miller of the Dee"—Hugh Lupus—The Plague in Cheshire—Ancient Eddisbury—St. Peter's Chains: an Old Congleton Custom—Was Mary Fitton Shakespeare's "Dark Lady"?—Sandbach Over Sixty Years Ago—Ancient Bridges, Fords, and Ferries—Cheshire Proverbial Phrases—A Souling Song—President Bradshaw—Thomas Parnell, Poet—Bishop Heber—Punishing Scolding Women—Index.

"Mr. William Andrews has produced a very attractive and interesting volume."—*Liverpool Post.*

"A high standard of literary merit is preserved throughout."—*Chester Courant.*

"The twenty-odd chapters which comprise this handsome volume are for the most part the productions of different authors, every one of whom has made a special study of the subject upon which he writes. As a result of this happy arrangement, a varied and entertaining, as well as a reliable and instructive, treatise of 'Bygone Cheshire' is presented."—*Liverpool Mercury.*

Bygone Nottinghamshire.

By WILLIAM STEVENSON.

Demy 8vo., Cloth gilt, 7s. 6d. Numerous Illustrations.

Contents :—The Wapentakes—The Origin of the County—The Origin of the Town—The Earliest Recorded Visitors to the County—The Suppression of the Knights Templars—Old Sanctuary Days—Notable Instances of Sanctuary—A Note on the Beverley Sanctuary—The King's Gallows of the County—The Reign of Terror in Notts.—Public Executions—Old Family Feuds—Visitations of the Plague—Visitation in the Town—Visitations in the County—Nottingham Goose Fair—The Great Priory Fair at Lenton—The Pilgrimage of Grace—The Pilgrim Fathers; or the Founders of New England—The Descendants of the Pilgrim Fathers—Archiepiscopal Palaces—The Ancient Inns and Taverns of Nottingham—Index.

"Mr. William Stevenson's book is a useful addition to the literature of the county, and in doing so we cheerfully offer a word of praise to the printer and publisher. Mr. William Andrews has done his part of the work admirably, and, seeing that he is a Notts. man, and himself an able and industrious antiquary, it must have been to him 'a labour of love.'"—*Newark Advertiser.*

"A most pleasant addition to local history."—*Nottingham Daily Guardian.*

www.ingramcontent.com/pod-product-compliance
Lightning Source LLC
Chambersburg PA
CBHW031902220426
43663CB00006B/736